Sew
Creative
Gifts
For Under $10™

Edited by Vicki Blizzard

HOUSE of
WHITE
BIRCHES
PUBLISHERS
SINCE 1947

Sew Creative Gifts for Under $10

Editor: Vicki Blizzard
Managing Editor: Barb Sprunger
Associate Editor: Kelly Keim
Technical Editor: Mary Jo Kurten
Book and Cover Design: Jessi Butler
Copy Editors: Nicki Lehman, Mary Martin
Publications Coordinator: Tanya Turner

Photography: Jeff Chilcote, Tammy Christian, Kelly Heydinger, Justin P. Wiard
Photography Assistant: Linda Quinlan

Production Coordinator: Brenda Gallmeyer
Production Artist: Ronda Bechinski
Production Assistant: Janet Bowers
Technical Artists: Leslie Brandt, Julie Catey, Chad Summers
Traffic Coordinator: Sandra Beres

Publishers: Carl H. Muselman, Arthur K. Muselman
Chief Executive Officer: John Robinson
Marketing Director: Scott Moss
Book Marketing Manager: Craig Scott
Product Development Director: Vivian Rothe
Publishing Services Manager: Brenda R. Wendling

Printed in the United States of America
First Printing: 2002
Library of Congress Number: 00-112317
ISBN: 1-882138-79-1

Every effort has been made to ensure the accuracy and completeness of the instructions
in this book. However, we cannot be responsible for human error or for the results when using
materials other than those specified in the instructions, or for variations in individual work.

Welcome!

Sometimes it seems like there are so many gift-giving occasions that it's hard to keep up with all of them. And when you have several birthdays in the same month (or week), it can wreak havoc with your time, not to mention your budget!

The projects we've chosen for this book were all designed to be sewn, start to finish, for under $10! How in the world did we do that, you might ask? Well, we gave our designers specific instructions to use fabrics found at garage sales, fabrics recycled from worn-out clothing, and buttons and embellishments removed from outgrown or out-of-date clothing. We then asked them to create wonderful projects that look like they've been made from brand-spanking-new fabrics and purchased by you at the finest boutique in town! We think they more than accomplished this task, and we hope you agree!

You can accomplish the same things they have, too, by using our patterns and following our easy instructions. These projects are all quick to make and will give you quite a sense of satisfaction when you have a finished piece in hand. You'll be especially happy to know that you've sewn beautiful gifts to give away or keep on hand for unexpected gift-giving occasions without breaking your budget!

We know you'll enjoy this book, and hope it's one you'll return to time and time again both for projects to make and for inspiration!

Until next time, happy stitching!

Vicki Blizzard

Editor

Contents

14

24

54

70

Gifts From the Heart

How do I love thee? Let me stitch the ways!

Heart sachets will remind a special girl that you love her every time she opens her drawer or closet door. Show the happy wedding couple how much you care about them with a sheet set you've stitched with love.

These gifts are so economical, you'll be looking for special ways to say "I love you" just to have an excuse to stitch one!

Hearts Entwined

By Holly Daniels

Linked hearts on bed linens make a perfect wedding gift. If you don't know the bride's colors, try a subtle beige-on-white combination. If someone is making a quilt for the bride, ask for matching scraps for the hearts.

Project Specifications

Skill Level: Beginner

Sheet Size: Any Size

Note: Directions are for twin sheet and pillowcase, but additional hearts can be added for any size.

Materials

- Twin sheet set—1 flat and 1 fitted sheet and one pillowcase
- Fabric scraps that coordinate with sheets
- 17" x 36" fusible transfer web
- 1 yard fabric stabilizer
- Air-soluble marker
- All purpose thread to match fabric scraps
- 4" x 4½" template material
- Basic sewing supplies and tools

Instructions

Step 1. Prewash sheets and fabrics; do not use fabric softener.

Step 2. Transfer heart to template material and cut out. Trace both inner and outer lines of 28 hearts on paper side of fusible transfer web leaving ½" space around each shape. Cut out, leaving approximately ¼" margin around each shape.

Step 3. Press fabric scraps. Following manufacturer's directions, fuse hearts to backs of selected fabric scraps. Each may be a different color or you may have several of each color. Cut out on both inner and outer traced lines, but do not cut slash line yet.

Step 4. Mark center of pillowcase hem with air-soluble marker. Lay out seven hearts across pillowcase hem, aligning center heart with center mark as shown in Fig. 1. First heart at far right will not be slashed. Slash remaining six hearts as shown on pattern. Slip first heart through slash and arrange so hearts appear to be interlocked. Continue to add hearts

working right to left in a straight line. When all hearts are arranged, fuse in place.

Step 5. Mark center of flat sheet with air-soluble marker. Place 21 hearts along top hem. Arrange and fuse in place as in Step 4.

Step 6. Cut fabric stabilizer to fit behind hearts. Stitch around each heart using matching thread and buttonhole- or zigzag-stitch. Remove stabilizer and trim threads.

Step 7. With a narrow satin stitch or decorative stitch, sew directly over factory-stitched hem. Trim threads. $

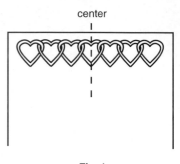

Fig. 1
Arrange 7 hearts on pillowcase as shown.

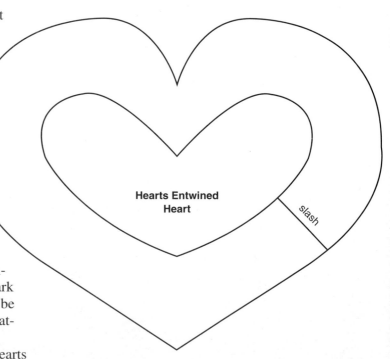

Hearts Entwined Heart

Vintage Valentine

By Mary Ayres

Combine your leftover upholstery or drapery fabric with some lace and silk fabric scraps to create a beautiful coordinated look for your home.

Project Specifications

Skill Level: Beginner

Pillow Size: 14" x 14" excluding ruffle

Materials

- 14" x 14" pillow form
- 12" x 12" Cluny-edge heart place mat
- 4"-long fabric and Battenburg lace heart doily
- 1 (⅞") flat button
- 8" x 8" square of silk fabric
- ½ yard solid or small-print fabric for center panel and pillow backing
- ¾ yard large-print fabric for border and ruffle
- 8" x 8" square of fusible transfer web
- 6-strand embroidery floss to match silk fabric
- Embroidery needle
- 2 tea bags
- Basic sewing supplies and tools

Instructions

Step 1. From solid or small-print fabric cut a background square 11¾" x 11¾".

Step 2. From large-print fabric cut two strips each 1⅞" x 11¾" and 1⅞" x 14½". Sew shorter strips to sides of background square and longer strips to top and bottom.

Step 3. Steep two tea bags in four cups of very hot water. Immerse place mat and doily in tea and dye to desired color. Machine-dry and press flat. Carefully cut fabric from inside place mat heart and Battenburg lace heart close to stitching.

Step 4. Fuse the square of fusible transfer web to back side of silk fabric following manufacturer's instructions. Place the right side of the place mat heart against the paper side of the fused silk heart. Draw around inside cut edge of place mat heart with pencil onto paper backing. Add ⅛" around drawn heart. Cut along outer line and peel off paper backing.

Step 5. Fuse silk heart to center of background panel. Pin place mat heart to center panel with inside edges overlapping edges of silk heart. Sew inside and outside edges of place mat heart to background panel using invisible stitches.

Step 6. Pin Battenburg lace heart to center of silk heart with top edges butting up against center of place mat heart. Sew inside and outside edges of Battenburg lace heart to center panel, using invisible stitches.

Step 7. Using 3 strands of embroidery floss embroider around inside and outside edges of Battenburg lace heart with stem stitch as shown in Fig. 1. Embroider around inner edge of place mat heart with buttonhole stitch as shown in Fig. 2.

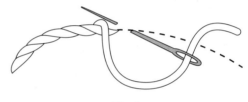

Fig. 1
Stem Stitch

Step 8. Sew button to center top of Battenburg lace heart with embroidery floss.

Step 9. From large-print fabric cut three 6" x 36" strips. Sew short ends together to form a ring. Fold strip in half lengthwise, wrong sides together.

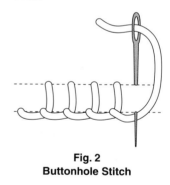

Fig. 2
Buttonhole Stitch

Step 10. Divide ring in four equal sections and mark with pins. Sew a basting stitch around ruffle close to raw edges, beginning and ending thread between each marked section. Pin ruffle to corners of pillow front at breaks in basting thread. Pull threads to gather, adjusting ruffles evenly on each side of pillow. Pin in place. Sew ruffle to pillow front.

Step 11. From solid or textured fabric cut a 14½" x 14½" square for pillow back. Right sides together, sew pillow front to pillow back, leaving a 10" opening at bottom. Trim corner seams and turn right side out. Insert pillow form and close opening with hand stitches. $

Cheery Checks Catch-All

By Chris Malone

Dress up an inexpensive container for presentation of whatever you may be giving—cookies, fruit, kitchen items or flowers. If made with items on hand it costs less than a purchased gift bag!

Project Specifications

Skill Level: Beginner

Catch-All Size: Approximately 5" x 10"

Note: Vary containers and make any size.

Materials

- Oatmeal box 5" x 9¾"
- ⅓ yard red-and-white check or plaid
- ¼ yard red-and-white print for bow and trim
- 5" x 10" red-and-white mini check for heart
- 2 (⅞") buttons
- Batting 16" x 9⅜"
- Fusible fleece
- All-purpose threads to match fabrics
- Buttonhole or carpet thread of any color
- Red cord or pearl cotton
- Polyester fiberfill
- Hot-glue gun and glue sticks
- Basic sewing supplies and tools

Instructions

Step 1. Measure container circumference and height. Do not include plastic rim at top if there is one. Multiply circumference by 2½ and cut a rectangle from red-and-white check that length and as wide as the height of the container. For example, the oatmeal box is 9⅜" in height, not including the plastic rim, and 16" in circumference; therefore, the rectangle is cut 9⅜" x 40". Right sides facing, sew the short ends together to form a tube; press seam open.

Step 2. Glue batting to outside of container, trimming if necessary to butt ends together smoothly.

Step 3. To gather red-and-white fabric tube made in Step 1, place a length of buttonhole or carpet thread ⅜" from one long edge. Machine-zigzag over thread with wide zigzag stitch; backstitch at start and finish. Be careful not to catch buttonhole or carpet thread in stitches. Repeat on other long edge.

Step 4. Slip tube over container and pull up heavy thread. Gather until fabric fits snugly around container

top and bottom. Knot and clip thread. Adjust gathers so folds run straight from top to bottom. Gently lift edges and apply dots of glue between fabric and container.

Step 5. Cut two fusible fleece strips ¾" x circumference of container. Remeasure circumference over fabric and batting. Cut two red-and-white print strips 1¾" wide and ½" longer than fleece strips. Fold in ¼" on long edges of fabric strips and place on work surface wrong side up.

Step 6. Place fusible fleece down center of fabric with fusible side up. Following manufacturer's directions, fold both edges of fabric over fleece and fuse to hold. Apply glue to one end of strip on wrong side and press to bottom edge of container, covering gathers. Glue just a few inches at a time going around container, gently pulling trim to fit snugly. Before gluing end of strip, check length and trim if necessary, peeling fabric back and cutting fleece, then re-covering with fabric. Butt ends together and whipstitch.

Step 7. Repeat Step 6 for top of container.

Step 8. For bow, cut a 6½" x 30" strip and a 2" x 3" rectangle from red-and-white print. Fold strip in half

Continued on page 21

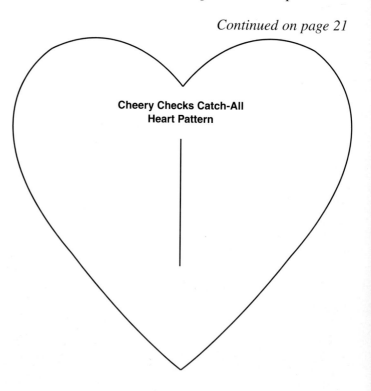

**Cheery Checks Catch-All
Heart Pattern**

Woven Heart Pillow

By Mary Ayres

Make this very quick and easy "love note" to express your sentiments to someone you care about.

Project Specifications

Skill Level: Beginner

Pillow Size: 14" x 14"

Materials

- ½ yard ticking-stripe fabric
- ⅛ yard each light and medium red stripe or plaid
- 1¾ yards jumbo black rickrack
- 14" x 14" pillow form
- 13" x 13" fusible transfer web
- Black 6-strand embroidery floss or pearl cotton
- Basic sewing supplies and tools

Instructions

Step 1. From light and medium red stripe or plaid cut 43 squares each 1½" x 1½". Be consistent with direction of stripe or plaid for each color.

Step 2. Following layout in Fig. 1, sew squares together. Sew horizontal rows and then sew rows together; press.

Step 3. Trace heart shape on paper side of fusible transfer web. Following manufacturer's directions, fuse to back of assembled squares. Again referring to Fig. 1, cut heart shape from fused squares.

Step 4. From ticking stripe cut two squares 14½" x 14½". Place heart shape right side up on one 14½" square and fuse.

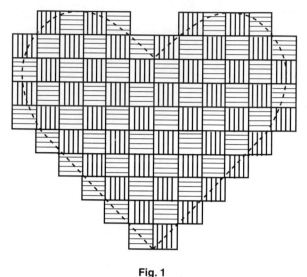

Fig. 1
Sew squares together as shown.

Step 5. With 3 strands of black embroidery floss or pearl cotton work buttonhole stitch around outside edge of heart.

Step 6. Stitching through center of rickrack, sew rickrack around pillow front ¼" from edge, beginning and ending in a bottom corner.

Step 7. Right sides together, sew pillow front and back together, leaving a 12" opening in bottom seam. Sew directly on rickrack stitching line. Trim corners and turn right side out.

Step 8. Insert pillow form and close opening with hand stitches. $

Sown With Love

By Angie Wilhite

Sow some seeds of kindness by making this loving gift for any gardener in your life. Because the pieces are small, you can probably find most of the materials in your scrap bag.

Project Specifications

Skill Level: Beginner

Wall Quilt Size: 16½" x 15"

Materials

- Tan print for background 12" x 13½"
- ⅛ yard blue print for borders
- Scraps of gold, navy, blue, tan, black, blue plaid, rust, rust plaid, green and gray for appliqué
- Scraps of black and white felt for eyes
- ⅓ yard fusible transfer web
- ⅛ yard heavy-duty fusible transfer web
- ¼ yard fusible interfacing
- ⅛ yard craft bond
- Fusible quilt batting 6" x 6"
- ⅓ yard tear-away fabric stabilizer
- Rotary-cutting tools
- 2 (⅝") plastic rings
- Backing 21" x 19"
- Thin batting 21" x 19"
- 1 package rust extra-wide double fold bias tape
- All-purpose threads to match fabrics
- Rayon machine-embroidery thread to match appliqué pieces
- 1 spool natural hand-quilting thread
- Black 6-strand embroidery floss
- Basic sewing supplies and tools

Instructions

Step 1. From blue print border fabric cut two strips each 2¼" x 13½" and 2¼" x 15½". Sew the shorter strips to the top and bottom of the tan background print piece. Sew the longer strips to the sides. Press seam allowances toward borders.

Step 2. Following manufacturer's directions, apply fusible quilt batting to selected navy hat fabric. Apply fusible interfacing to light-colored appliqué fabrics. Apply heavy-duty fusible transfer web to back of a 5" x 5" square of gold corner-heart fabric, and to black and white felt scraps. Apply craft bond to back of a 4" x 4" blue square selected for corner circles to be placed on corner hearts.

Step 3. Trace appliqué shapes on paper side of fusible transfer web. Cut out pieces on traced lines.

Step 4. Referring to photo, arrange appliqué pieces on tan background and gold hearts on four corners of border. Fuse in place.

Step 5. Referring to photo, work buttonhole stitch around hands, feet, ears, eyes, nose and snout with 2 strands of black embroidery floss.

Step 6. Pin or baste fabric stabilizer to back of design area. Using rayon embroidery thread in needle and all-purpose thread in bobbin, machine-satin-stitch around all appliqué pieces except bear head and gold corner hearts. Begin with pieces that appear to be near the back of the design and work forward.

Step 7. From the craft-bonded blue fabric, cut four corner circles. With matching thread tack each circle in the center of a gold corner heart.

Step 8. With 2 strands of black embroidery floss, work buttonhole stitch around bear head.

Step 9. Place backing fabric face down on work surface. Top with thin batting. Place appliquéd piece face up on top. Baste layers together.

Step 10. Hand-quilt around appliqué shapes and in the ditch on seam lines.

Step 11. Trim batting and backing even with quilt top. Bind with rust bias tape to finish.

Step 12. Sew plastic rings to top corners on back of quilt for hanging. $

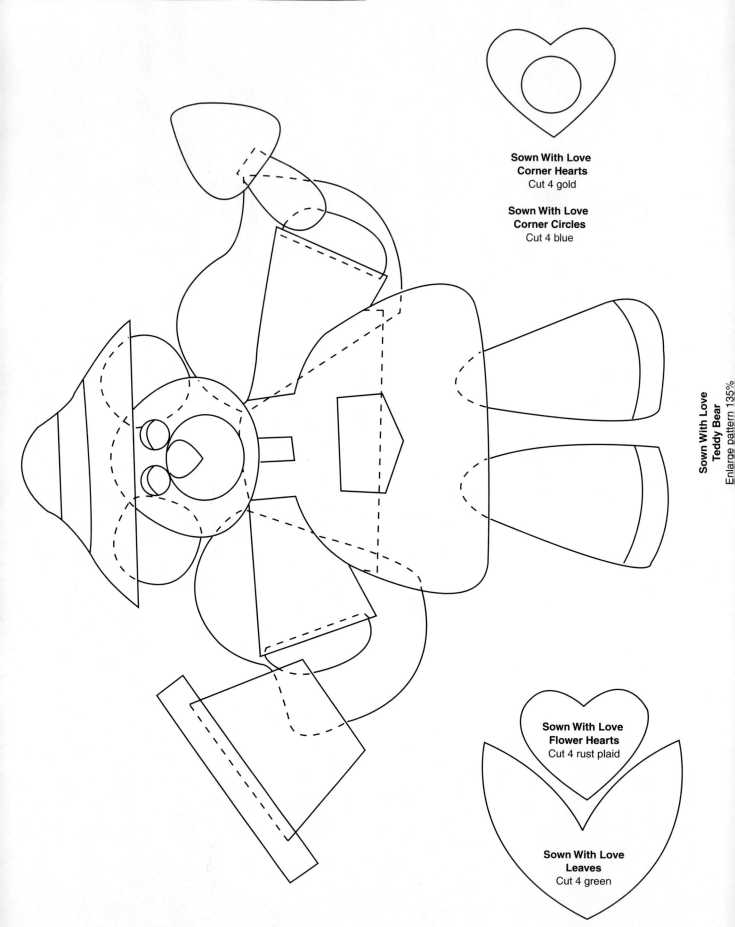

**Sown With Love
Corner Hearts**
Cut 4 gold

**Sown With Love
Corner Circles**
Cut 4 blue

**Sown With Love
Teddy Bear**
Enlarge pattern 135%

**Sown With Love
Flower Hearts**
Cut 4 rust plaid

**Sown With Love
Leaves**
Cut 4 green

Heirloom Lace Pillow

By Karen Mead

Do you have a pretty, lacy blouse in your closet that has outlived today's fashion, but because it has sentimental value you can't bear to discard it? Here's a perfect use for it.

Project Specifications

Skill Level: Beginner

Pillow Size: Any size

Note: Size will vary depending on size of fabric pieces cut from blouse.

Materials

- Pretty, lace-trimmed blouse ready for recycling
- 1 yard muslin for lining
- Polyester fiberfill
- Basic sewing supplies and tools

Instructions

Step 1. Place blouse on flat work surface and cut off under arms—cutting through front and back of garment. Cut square or rectangle from lower section so that bottom seam and side seams are not included in area, as shown in Fig. 1.

Step 2. Stitch along front placket to keep blouse front closed securely.

Step 3. Rearrange buttons if necessary to center them.

Step 4. Cut two muslin pieces same size as blouse pieces.

Step 5. With right side of blouse pieces facing, pin lining pieces to the wrong sides of each piece. Stitch around all four sides, leaving 4" opening for turning and stuffing. Clip corners and turn right side out.

Step 6. Stuff pillow with polyester fiberfill and close opening with hand stitches. $

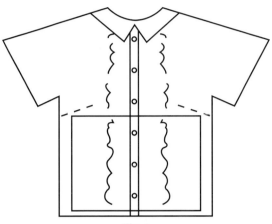

Fig. 1
Cut square or rectangle as shown.

Buttoned-Up Heart Sachets

By Mary Ayres

Made in red and off-white, these sachets are perfect little valentines, but they are beautiful in any color—just choose a monochromatic scheme for all the materials for each sachet.

Project Specifications

Skill Level: Beginner

Sachet Size: Approximately 3" x 3" plus tassels

Note: Instructions are for red sachet. You may substitute any color of your choice.

Materials

- 2 squares red fabric 3½" x 3½"
- 19–22 (⅜"–⅝") flat red buttons
- 3½" red tassel
- 6-strand red embroidery floss
- 14" narrow red piping
- 4" (⅛"-wide) red satin ribbon
- 1 paper sachet
- All-purpose red thread
- Funnel (optional)
- Basic sewing supplies and tools

Instructions

Step 1. Transfer heart pattern to right side of one red fabric square for sachet top. Referring to Fig. 1 and using 3 strands of red embroidery floss, work stem stitch around heart.

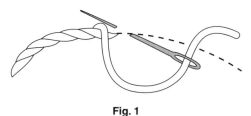

Fig. 1
Stem Stitch

Step 2. With red embroidery floss, sew buttons inside heart, filling entire heart shape.

Step 3. Sew red piping around sachet top ¼" from edge, raw edges aligned. Start and stop in top corner. Clip piping seam at corners.

Step 4. Fold ribbon in half, end to end, and baste to top corner of sachet, raw edges aligned.

Step 5. Right sides together, sew sachet front and back together along piping stitching. Leave 1½" opening along one side. Trim corners and turn right side out.

Step 6. Fill square firmly with paper sachet. For convenient filling, insert funnel in fabric opening and pour sachet through the funnel.

Step 7. Close opening with hand stitches.

Step 8. With red embroidery floss, sew a button in the top corner of sachet; sew cord end of tassel to back of bottom lower corner. $

**Buttoned-Up Heart Sachets
Heart Pattern**

3½" fabric square

Cheery Checks Catch-All
Continued from page 12

lengthwise, right sides together, and sew along edges, leaving a 4" opening for turning. Sew a 2" V at each end as shown in Fig. 1. Trim corners and turn right side out. Close opening with hand stitches.

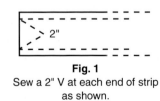

Fig. 1
Sew a 2" V at each end of strip
as shown.

Step 9. Fold strip into bow shape with 3" loops. Wrap thread around center to hold. Fold long sides of small rectangle in toward center to make a 1" x 2" strip. Fold this strip around center of bow, overlapping ends in back. Glue to secure.

Step 10. Fold 5" x 10" red-and-white, mini-check piece in half, right sides together. Trace heart pattern on one side of doubled fabric. Sew all around on traced line. Trim seam and clip curves. Cut a slash through one layer only. Turn heart right side out through slash. Stuff evenly with polyester fiberfill and close opening with hand stitches.

Step 11. With white thread, sew a button on each side of heart, pulling thread gently to indent heart. Wrap one end of red cord around button on back of heart (slashed side). Tie cord in a knot with knot toward top of heart. Trim other end of cord to 5". Apply a spot of glue to trim at top of container. Place cord in glue and cover end of red cord with center of bow. $

Birthday Wishes

Make a wish—blow out the candles! Who wouldn't wish for a gift like one of these?

From gift bags to soft toys, these fun gifts won't break your budget. Youngsters will enjoy the play stage and puppets this year and for years to come. The young-at-heart will enjoy the Double-Dip Delight necklace. Make one for your mom and watch her smile every time she wears it!

Whether you stitch one for a special birthday celebration, or stitch several to keep on hand for last-minute party invitations, these gifts are sure to please!

Now Playing–
A Party Just for You!

By Lisa Galvin

This self-contained take-along project will provide hours of creativity and fun. Present the stage at a party and let each child make a pencil-top puppet for an original production and take-home party favor.

Project Specifications

Skill Level: Beginner

Size: Adult-size shoe box

Materials

- 1 adult-size shoe box
- ½ yard brightly colored print fabric
- ½ yard brightly colored striped fabric
- ½ yard unbleached muslin
- 2 (¾") wooden dowel rods
- 1 (¼") wooden dowel rod
- 3 wooden yellow lead pencils
- Scraps of polyester fiberfill
- 1 sheet black construction paper
- White crayon or chalk
- Craft glue
- Toothpick
- Embroidery needle
- Fine-line permanent black marker
- Solid piece of plastic foam packing material to fit shoe box lid
- Scraps of corrugated cardboard
- Sandpaper
- Scraps of fabric, ribbon, beads, lace, rickrack, elastic, sequins, snaps and embroidery floss to embellish puppets
- Basic sewing supplies and tools

Clown Puppet 1

- Green yarn
- Black 6-strand embroidery floss
- 1 (¼") snap
- 4 (5mm) red sequins
- 6½" piece of ¾"-wide lace
- 12" piece of elastic beading cord, embroidery floss, string or ribbon

Clown Puppet 2

- Red yarn
- 6" x 4" scrap of fabric for wizard hat
- 2 black beads
- Purple embroidery floss
- Scrap of red felt
- Small jingle bell
- 12" piece of ⅛"-wide satin ribbon
- ⅜" red pompom
- 4" scrap of ¼"-wide elastic

Clown Puppet 3

- Yellow yarn
- Purple and yellow embroidery floss
- ⅜" green pompom
- Red bead
- 4" x 4" piece of ribbing from old sock
- 2½" x 3" scrap of denim

Instructions

Stage

Note: If selected fabric has light background it may be necessary to cover shoe box with white paper prior to covering to prevent see-through.

Step 1. Measure box width and length. Measure height and multiply times 2. Add this figure to both length and width. Add 3" to each of these dimensions. Use these two measurements to cut brightly colored print fabric to cover box.

Step 2. Repeat Step 1 for fabric to cover lid, but add only 2" (instead of 3").

Step 3. Wrap box and lid neatly as if wrapping a gift; sides first, then ends. Glue excess fabric to inner edge of each piece to hold securely in place. It may be necessary to trim away some excess fabric on ends to lie flat.

Step 4. Cut plastic foam packing material to fit comfortably inside box lid, leaving about ¼" space on each side. Clip a ⅜" square from each corner as shown in Fig. 1 to create cavities for ¾" dowel posts. Glue to inside of lid.

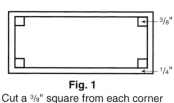

Fig. 1
Cut a ⅜" square from each corner of plastic foam.

Step 5. Cut ¾" dowel rods into four equal 13" lengths. Check to be sure dowel rods will fit diagonally inside box for storage. If not, trim them to fit. Lightly sand to smooth rough ends.

Step 6. From corrugated cardboard scraps cut four post holders (see page 33). Referring to Fig. 2, fold on dashed lines. Glue top tabs together. Use tape to hold them together while glue is drying. Glue post holders in place at each of four box corners. Set aside to dry. *Note: Holders should be placed 1/4" down from top edge with folded-in flaps towards bottom of box.*

Box bottom

Box opening

Fig. 2
Fold post holders and glue in box corners as shown.

Backdrop Curtain

Step 1. From unbleached muslin cut a rectangle 15" x shoe box length plus 4½". Fold under all sides ½" and press. Stitch ¼" from edge on all sides. Fold under 1¼" along one long edge and press. Stitch ⅛" from fold. Stitch ⅝" from same fold to create a rod pocket for dowel. With fingers, pinch-pleat curtain at 1" intervals top and bottom. Press well and unfold to reveal pleats.

Step 2. From ¼" dowel rod, cut two pieces the length of the box. Slip one rod through the backdrop-curtain rod pocket, gathering on rod and leaving 1" of exposed rod on each end.

Stage Curtains

Step 1. From brightly colored striped fabric cut two pieces each 15" x 8", with the stripe running lengthwise. Turn under all sides ¼" and press. Stitch ⅛" from edge. Fold under 1¼" along one 8" edge of each piece and press. Stitch ⅛" from fold and then ⅝" from same fold to create rod pockets. Pleat as in backdrop curtain; press. Slip both pieces onto remaining dowel rod leaving 1" of rod exposed at each end.

Corner Posts

Step 1. From brightly colored striped fabric cut four

pieces 13" x 3". Fold under ½" on 3" ends and press. Stitch ¼" from fold. With right sides together fold each piece in half lengthwise. Stitch ¼" from raw edge to create four tubes open on each end.

Step 2. Turn tubes right side out and slip one over each of the four ¾" dowel rods.

Step 3. Slip one covered corner post into each cardboard post holder in box. Slip other end of each corner post into corner cavities of box lid to create stage as shown in Fig. 3.

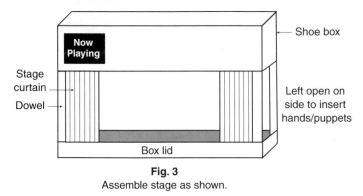
Fig. 3
Assemble stage as shown.

Step 4. Hang backdrop curtain and stage curtains on exposed edges of corner post holders, front and back. Stage curtains can slide to center for a closed position or be pulled to each side and tied. Sides are left open for inserting puppets.

Marquee

Step 1. From black construction paper cut one piece 4" x 2½". With chalk or white crayon write "Now Playing." If using chalk, spray with hair spray to prevent smudging. Glue to side of box as shown in Fig. 3. If desired, add rickrack or other trim around edges.

Step 2. Cut another piece of black construction paper 9" x 5½". Bring short ends together and fold in half. With white crayon or chalk write "A Party Just for You" as shown in Fig. 4. The child's name may be inserted on the sign. Add rickrack or trim to decorate the marquee.

Fig. 4
Letter marquee as shown.

Puppet Heads

Note: Puppets can be made as shown or challenge children to create their own.

Step 1. From unbleached muslin cut a square 8" x 8". Fold in half. Beginning ½" from one end, with pencil trace three clown puppet heads directly onto muslin, leaving 1" between each. Beginning and ending at dots and sewing through double layers, machine-stitch directly on traced lines. Turn each head right side out.

Step 2. Grasp flap ends at bottom of head and with unsharpened pencil stuff head with fiberfill. Insert flaps as well as eraser end of pencil. Twist pencil to work its way into head. Redistribute fiberfill as needed. Add a drop of glue into bottom opening. Twist pencil one more time to distribute glue evenly to make head adhere to pencil. Whipstitch opening closed. Repeat for three heads.

Clown Puppet 1

Step 1. With black embroidery floss cross-stitch X's for eyes as shown in Fig. 5. Bring knotted ends of thread in and out of top of head where hair will later conceal them.

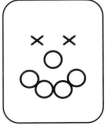
Fig. 5
Clown Puppet 1.

Step 2. With toothpick and glue place dots of glue in desired areas for nose and mouth. Add snap for nose and four red sequins for mouth.

Step 3. Glue strands of yarn to head for hair. Yarn raveled from a knitted or crocheted piece gives a great curly look.

Step 4. From brightly colored striped fabric cut a piece 6" x 2" to make collar. Turn under each 6" side ¼". Stitch ⅛" from fold. Bring 2" ends together, right sides facing; stitch ¼" from edge.

Step 5. Starting at seam, stitch or glue ¾" lace to wrong side of one edge of collar, overlapping at starting point. At a point opposite the seam ¼" from one edge, lay 12" piece of elastic beading cord (or trim of choice) onto fabric. Zigzag-stitch over it, keeping cord in center so it remains free and can be moved back and forth. Pull cords to gather. Slip onto pencil and tie a knot and then a bow with ends of cord. Apply glue to pencil at neck, slide collar over glue and hold until secure.

Clown Puppet 2

Step 1. With purple embroidery floss cross-stitch X for nose as shown in Figure 6. Bring knotted ends of thread in and out of top of head where hair will later conceal them.

Step 2. Use Clown 2 Mouth pattern to trace mouth on red felt. Draw a smile on felt with fine-line permanent black marker. Glue mouth to face and use marker to make cheek lines at each side of mouth.

Step 3. Using Clown 2 Wizard Hat pattern, trace and cut as directed. Right sides together, stitch hat pieces together. Turn right side out. Press under a ½" hem at bottom. Stitch elastic to bottom edge ¼" from pressed fold, stretching to fit. Stitch pompom to point of hat.

Step 4. Wrap red yarn around two fingers 10–12 times as shown in Fig. 7. With a 6" piece of yarn tie a knot around all yarn between fingers again referring to Fig. 7. Slip off fingers and clip all yarn loops. Make two bundles. Glue one bundle side to side on puppet head. Glue second bundle front to back.

Step 5. Drop jingle bell into hat so that it remains free to bounce and jingle with the hat. Glue hat to head.

Step 6. Wrap ribbon around pencil and tie a bow. Apply a drop of glue at neck, slide ribbon onto it to hold in place.

Clown Puppet 3

Step 1. Fold sock ribbing in half and stitch ¼" from long raw edges. Hand-baste one open end, pull to gather and knot. Turn right side out. Repeat on other open end. Tuck end into hat bringing gathered ends together. Fold up open end creating a stocking cap.

Step 2. Trace and cut Clown 3 Collar as directed on pattern. With yellow embroidery floss stitch X's as indicated on pattern. Fold in half and cut a small X at the center creating a neck opening. Slide collar onto pencil through opening. Glue to pencil at neck.

Step 3. With purple embroidery floss, stitch eyes as shown in Fig. 8. Sew on red bead for mouth and

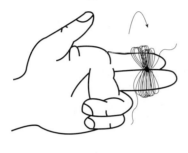

Fig. 6
Clown Puppet 2.

Fig. 7
Wrap yarn around fingers as shown.

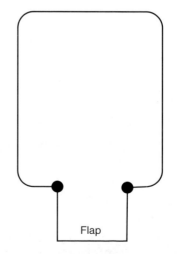

Fig. 8
Clown Puppet 3.

glue on green pompom for nose. From yellow yarn make four hair bundles as shown in Step 4, Clown Puppet 2. Glue to head. Glue stocking cap to hair. $

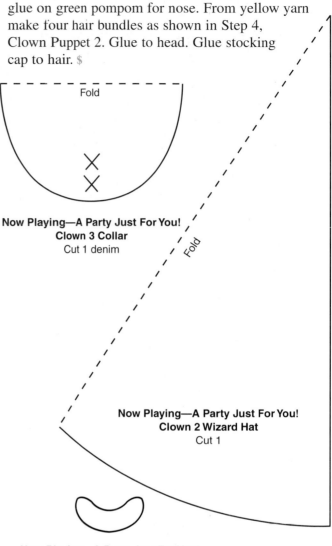

Now Playing—A Party Just For You!
Clown 3 Collar
Cut 1 denim

Fold

Now Playing—A Party Just For You!
Clown 2 Wizard Hat
Cut 1

Now Playing—A Party Just For You!
Clown 2 Mouth
Cut 1 red felt

Flap

Now Playing—A Party Just For You!
Clown Puppet Head

Patterns continued on page 33

Birthday Boy & Birthday Girl Gift Bags

By Chris Malone

All the materials for these adorable bags were found in the designer's scrap bag. Examine your own stash and substitute colors and trims with those you have on hand.

Project Specifications

Skill Level: Beginner

Bag Size: Approximately 3½" x 7"

Note: Materials listed will make one boy and one girl bag.

Materials

- ⅛ yard black-and-white striped fabric
- 4½" x 2¾" scrap of solid black fabric
- Scraps of orange, black, light pink and dark pink felt
- Orange, black and dark pink 6-strand embroidery floss
- 4¼" x 2½" scrap of fusible transfer web
- 8" (⅝"-wide) orange grosgrain ribbon
- Two 4" lengths (⅜"-wide) multicolored-stripe grosgrain ribbon
- 12" (⅝"-wide) black-and-white dot grosgrain ribbon
- 18" each (⅜"-wide) dark blue and lime green grosgrain ribbon
- 3" (⅜"-wide) blue-and-white dot grosgrain ribbon
- 4" (⅜"-wide) yellow-and-white dot grosgrain ribbon
- 4" (1½"-wide) white gathered lace eyelet
- 1 (½") miniature brass buckle
- 2 (⅜") white buttons
- 1½ yards yellow acrylic yarn
- 12" brown acrylic yarn
- Size 5 aluminum knitting needle
- 4 (5mm) black half-beads
- Seam sealant
- Fabric glue
- Transparent or masking tape
- Wire snips
- Basic sewing supplies and tools

Instructions

Girl Bag

Step 1. From black-and-white striped fabric cut four 4" x 6" rectangles.

Step 2. Cut legs, arms, head and cheeks as directed on patterns.

Step 3. With 2 strands of black embroidery floss buttonhole-stitch two leg pieces together. Repeat for second leg. Repeat with orange floss for arms.

Step 4. For bag front, place white lace eyelet right side up on one black-and-white rectangle with bottom of lace ⅜" above one short end. Place a 4" length of orange grosgrain ribbon over top gathered edge of lace. Center yellow-and-white dot ribbon on top of orange ribbon. Glue or stitch in place. Glue or stitch ⅜"-wide multicolored-stripe grosgrain ribbon ⅛" above orange ribbon.

Step 5. Pin arms on each side of bag front with top of arm 2¼" down from top of bag and straight edge aligned with sides of bag. Pin legs to bottom of bag with ⅜" space between legs and straight edges aligned with bag bottom. Baste in place.

Step 6. To line bag, sew top of bag front to short end of another fabric rectangle, right sides together. Repeat with remaining two rectangles. Press seams open and pin pairs right sides together, matching seam lines. Sew around rectangle leaving a 2" opening along one edge of lining. Trim corners and turn right side out through opening. Close opening with hand stitches and tuck lining into bag.

Step 7. Cut two 3" pieces of black-and-white dot grosgrain ribbon for casing. Apply seam sealant to cut ends and allow to dry. Place one ribbon just below top of bag front, centered between side seams. Topstitch on long edges, sewing through bag front and front lining only. Repeat for bag back.

Step 8. Glue small cheek circles to face circle. With dark pink embroidery floss, stitch a small V for a mouth. Glue two half-beads in place for eyes. Glue face to bag front with top of head 1" down from top of bag.

Step 9. Referring to photo for placement, sew two white buttons to bag front.

Step 10. For hair, wrap yellow yarn around knitting needle, securing ends with tape. Place needle in a 275-degree oven for 15 minutes. Allow to cool. Remove from needle. Referring to photo, arrange and glue hair around face.

Step 11. Thread ⅜"-wide lime green grosgrain ribbon through casing. To close bag, pull ribbon and tie ends.

Boy Bag

Step 1. Repeat Girl Bag Steps 1–3.

Step 2. Trace a 4" x 2¼" rectangle on paper side of

fusible transfer web. Cut out leaving a narrow margin around traced lines. Following manufacturer's instructions, fuse to black fabric rectangle. Cut out on traced lines. Fuse rectangle to right side of one end of one black-and-white striped rectangle. With white thread, hand- or machine-stitch a line 1¼" long up from bottom of pants at center.

Step 3. Place 4" piece of ⅝"-wide orange grosgrain ribbon over top of pants. Topstitch.

Step 4. With wire snips remove prong from buckle

Continued on page 33

Birthday Cupcake Surprise Bag

By June Fiechter

*This whimsical but sturdy little bag holds a lot and could play many roles.
Use it as a craft supply holder, a party table decoration or favor (fill it with candy)
or a tote bag for toys to get little tykes through those long waits at restaurants.*

Project Specifications

Skill Level: Beginner

Bag Size: Approximately 8" x 8"

Materials

- Wheat-colored felt circle 11" in diameter
- Pink felt 8" x 30"
- 32" cotton drawstring cord (salvage from an old sweatshirt)
- Red yarn pompom made from scrap yarn
- Kreative Kanvas from Kunin 4¾" x 15" and a 4½" circle
- All-purpose threads to match felt
- Fabric glue
- Basic sewing supplies and tools

Instructions

Step 1. Measure and mark every 1¾" around outer edge of wheat-colored felt circle and draw a circle 4½" in diameter in the center as shown in Fig. 1. Place a dot in the center of the circle.

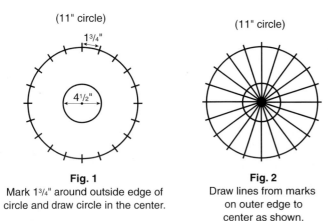

Fig. 1
Mark 1¾" around outside edge of circle and draw circle in the center.

Fig. 2
Draw lines from marks on outer edge to center as shown.

Step 2. Draw lines from outer-edge marks to center dot to create a spoke effect as shown in Fig. 2.

Step 3. Create ¼" darts, folding on marked lines. Start at outer edge of center circle and gradually increase width of dart to ¼" at outer edge of 11" circle as shown in Fig. 3. Turn right side out to form cupcake holder.

Fig. 3
Sew darts as shown.

Step 4. Bring short ends of Kreative Kanvas rectangle together and place inside cupcake holder. Adjust ends to fit snugly. Remove cylinder and stitch to hold this exact size. Measure down 1½" from top of cylinder and draw a line all the way around.

Step 5. Bring the short ends of the pink felt rectangle together to create a cylinder shape. Sew ends together as shown in Fig. 4. Do not turn right side out. Sew a long running stitch around the bottom of the cylinder. Pull up to gather, but do not knot.

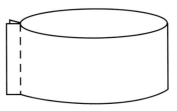

Fig. 4
Make felt cylinder as shown and stitch.

Step 6. Pull felt cylinder up over Kreative Kanvas cylinder just to marked line. Pull threads to tighten gathers around Kanvas cylinder and stitch in place. Pull felt up right side out as shown in Fig. 5.

Step 7. Sew a ½" casing around the top of the pink felt cylinder. Clip a small hole in the casing on the outer side only. Run the cotton cord through the casing. Tie a knot at each end. Leave ungathered to continue work.

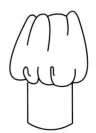

Fig. 5
Pull felt up and away from cupcake holder as shown.

Step 8. Apply fabric glue to one side of 4½" Kreative Kanvas circle. Place glue side down inside bottom of cupcake holder.

Continued on page 33

Patched-Up Heart

By Janna Britton

Could there be special significance in offering the one you love a patched-up heart?
Only the two of you will know, but the message may be important!

Project Specifications

Skill Level: Beginner

Pillow Size: Approximately 19" x 19" including fringe

Materials

- Worn men's jeans 34 x 32 or larger
- Scraps of assorted old denims
- White all-purpose thread
- Rotary-cutting tools
- Polyester fiberfill
- Basic sewing supplies and tools

Instructions

Step 1. From men's jeans cut a pillow backing piece 22" x 19½". Cut from the widest part of the thigh with a seam running down the middle of the 22" width.

Step 2. From men's jeans cut two strips 2½" x 25". Tack together loosely to make one long strip.

Step 3. From denim scraps cut 34 square 3" x 3", using a variety of dark and light colors. Following lay-out in Fig. 1, sew squares together. First sew in horizontal rows and then sew rows together.

Step 4. Lay out patched piece as flat as possible and cut heart shape as shown in Fig. 1.

Step 5. Place patched heart on backing piece and cut heart 2" larger all around.

Step 6. Pin strip made in Step 2 to outer edges of backing heart, wrong sides together. Place patched heart on top, seamed side up. Stitch around patched heart, ¼" from edge, leaving a 3" opening on one side for stuffing.

Step 7. With scissors, snip backing and strip at ¼" intervals as shown in Fig. 2.

Step 8. Machine-wash and dry pillow to create frayed fringe and seams. Clean the dryer lint trap half-way through drying cycle as a safety measure.

Step 9. Stuff pillow with polyester fiberfill and close opening with hand stitches. $

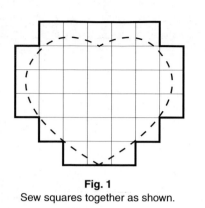

Fig. 1
Sew squares together as shown.

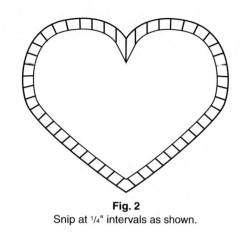

Fig. 2
Snip at ¼" intervals as shown.

Now Playing—A Party Just for You!
Continued from page 27

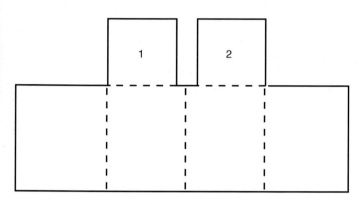

Now Playing—A Party Just For You!
Post Holder
Cut 4 cardboard

Birthday Cupcake Surprise Bag
Continued from page 30

Step 9. Slide Kanvas cylinder down into cupcake holder and apply fabric glue around bottom edge to attach it to the bottom Kanvas circle.

Step 10. Use fabric glue to attach red yarn pompom to pink felt just above the cord entrance, being careful not to obstruct cord movement.

Step 11. Place a dot of fabric glue at the top of each cupcake-holder dart to fasten it to the pink felt icing. $

Birthday Boy & Birthday Girl Gift Bags
Continued from page 29

and thread it onto 4" piece of ⅜"-wide multicolored-stripe grosgrain ribbon. Glue or stitch in place. Center over orange ribbon and glue or stitch in place.

Step 5. Repeat Steps 5–8 of Girl Bag. Repeat Step 10 for hair, substituting brown yarn.

Step 6. Fold blue-and-white dot grosgrain ribbon into a bow shape. Wrap thread around middle of bow and glue to bag front under face for bow tie.

Step 7. Thread ⅜"-wide dark blue grosgrain ribbon through casing. To close bag, pull ribbon and tie ends. $

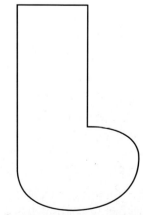

Birthday Boy & Birthday Girl Gift Bags
Boy Head—Cut 1 light pink felt
Girl Head—Cut 1 light pink felt

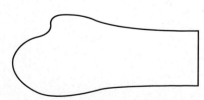

Birthday Boy & Birthday Girl Gift Bags
Boy Arm—Cut 4 orange felt
Girl Arm—Cut 4 orange felt

Birthday Boy & Birthday Girl Gift Bags
Boy Cheeks—Cut 2 dark pink felt
Girl Cheeks—Cut 2 dark pink felt

Birthday Boy & Birthday Girl Gift Bags
Boy Leg—Cut 4 black felt
Girl Leg—Cut 4 black felt

Pocketful of Love

By Cindy Gorder

An endless variety of objects—coins, keys, tiny gifts or keepsakes— can be tucked away in this stylized, silky heart.

Project Specifications

Skill Level: Beginner

Heart Size: Approximately 2¾" x 4" plus 38" beaded necklace

Materials

- 4" x 4½" scrap of sheer fabric such as organza
- 3 scraps of satin fabric 4" x 4½" for backing and lining
- 1½" x 2" scrap of velvet
- 1½" x 2" scrap of fusible transfer web
- 2 flea-market necklaces to take apart for pearls and large beads
- 1 (⅝") heart-shaped button
- 1½ yards metallic purple #8 fine thread
- Approximately 450 frosted clear glass size 11 seed beads
- Approximately 60 pink silver-lined size 6 seed beads
- Approximately 20 pink silver-lined size 11 seed beads
- 4 yards beading thread
- Beading and embroidery needles
- Basic sewing supplies and tools

Instructions

Step 1. Cut large hearts as directed on pattern.

Step 2. Trace small heart on paper side of fusible transfer web. Cut out, leaving ¼" margin around traced lines. Following manufacturer's directions, fuse to velvet scrap.

Step 3. Cut heart on traced lines and fuse to organza heart.

Step 4. With wrong side of heart lining to right side of organza heart, stitch around heart, leaving open between dots. Clip curves and turn right side out. Close opening with hand stitches.

Step 5. Stitch size 11 pink seed beads around perimeter of velvet heart. Sew heart-shaped button to center of velvet heart.

Step 6. Right sides together, stitch around heart back

and lining leaving open between dots. Clip curves and turn right side out. Close opening with hand stitches. Press edges of heart front and back. Avoid touching iron to velvet heart.

Step 7. Pin front and back hearts together. Buttonhole-stitch along top edge of front heart between triangles using purple metallic thread. Below triangles marked on pattern, take the buttonhole stitch through heart back as well as front and continue around the front and back to connect them.

Step 8. Stitch a frosted clear seed bead at the end of each buttonhole stitch as shown in Fig. 1.

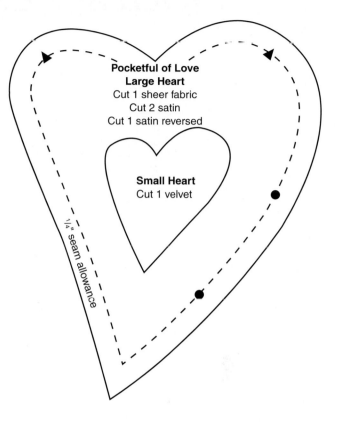

Pocketful of Love
Large Heart
Cut 1 sheer fabric
Cut 2 satin
Cut 1 satin reversed

Small Heart
Cut 1 velvet

¼" seam allowance

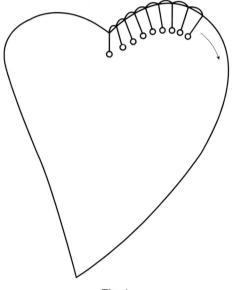

Fig. 1
Stitch a frosted clear seed bead at the
end of each buttonhole stitch as shown.

Step 9. For necklace cut a 43" length of beading thread and anchor to one triangle. String on two pearls, a large glass bead and another pearl. The next section consists of 10 frosted seed beads, then a size 6 pink. Repeat section five times.

Step 10. Add a decorative bead or larger pearl and a size 6 pink seed bead. Then five more repeats of 10 frosted seed beads followed by a pink size 6 seed bead. Add another decorative bead or larger pearl and a size 6 pink followed by 10 frosted and another pink. Alternate three pearls with three pink size 6. Repeat three more sections of 10 frosted clear followed by a size 6 pink. Again, add three pearls alternating with three pinks. Repeat three sections of 10 frosted clear followed by a size 6 pink.

Step 11. Alternate nine pearls with frosted clear seed beads, or as many as needed to make a 19" beaded

length. Place a size 6 pink at center back for reference. Repeat beading sequence in reverse for second half of necklace. Anchor securely to heart at other triangle.

Step 12. Reinforce necklace by cutting a second strand of beading thread and running through the beads the other direction, anchoring to heart at both ends.

Step 13. At bottom of heart anchor 36" length of beading thread and string on a pearl, size 6 pink, large decorative bead, another size 6 pink followed by a large decorative bead. Add a frosted clear seed bead and then take the needle back through the first beads and secure to the bottom of the heart. Go back through the strung beads again and add a few frosted clears, a size 6 pink and another frosted clear.

Step 14. Go back through the frosteds; bring needle out and double back through one frosted, then add several more and then a pink, and so on, making several strands of vary-

Fig. 2
Make several bead strands to form
tassel as shown.

ing lengths to form a tassel as shown in Fig. 2. Take needle back through all beads to bottom of heart and anchor to heart securely. $

Double-Dip Delight

By Debbie Roney

There are no age restrictions for ice cream! Young and old will love strands of these frosty delights designed in any flavor.

Project Specifications

Skill Level: Beginner

Necklace Size: Any size

Note: The number of cones and beads you string is your choice.

Materials

- Scraps of assorted fabrics for ice cream and beads
- Scraps of fabrics for cones
- All-purpose threads to match fabrics
- 6-strand embroidery floss or pearl cotton on which to string cones
- White yarn for stuffing
- Hand-sewing and embroidery needles.
- Plastic template material
- Small pointed tool for stuffing
- Basic sewing supplies and tools

Instructions

Designer Notes:

• Make chocolate chip scoops by dotting white fabric with fine-line brown permanent marker.

• Swirl flavors with pastel markers.

• Enhance colors of ice cream by using same color of yarn for stuffing.

Step 1. Trace and cut desired number of large cones from cone fabric. Bring right sides of straight edges together. Hand-stitch from bottom tip to top on stitching lines. At top edge, continue around top of cone with doubled thread and running stitch. Do not fasten off.

Step 2. Stuff cone with 2½"–3" of yarn. Draw up and secure thread, but do not cut. Leave needle threaded.

Step 3. Trace and cut two large ice cream scoops per cone. Work a running stitch on gathering line. Draw up thread and stuff with about 3" of yarn. Tie off and cut thread.

Step 4. Using threaded needle on cone, attach scoop to cone. Tie off and cut thread.

Step 5. Make a second scoop as in Step 3, but do not cut thread. Use uncut thread to attach second scoop to first scoop.

Step 6. Trace, cut and sew two small cones and four small scoops as in Steps 1–5.

Step 7. From selected fabrics trace enough beads to alternate with large cones. Work a running stitch on gathering line. Draw up, tucking raw edges in as you go. Pull up as tightly as you can and tie off.

Step 8. Measure the length you would like your necklace to be and add 5". Cut this length from 6-strand embroidery floss or pearl cotton.

Step 9. With embroidery needle, string large ice cream cones alternately with beads. Tie ends at the length you desire. Thread each loose end on embroidery needle and sew a small ice cream cone to each end as shown in Fig. 1. $

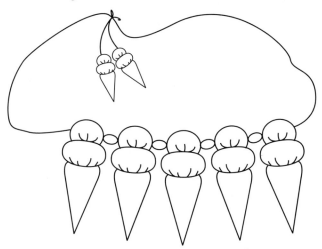

Fig. 1
Sew a small ice cream cone to each end
as shown.

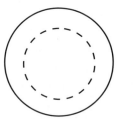

**Double-Dip Delight
Bead**

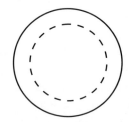

**Double-Dip Delight
Small Scoop**

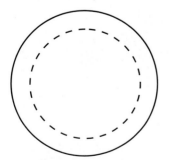

Double-Dip Delight
Large Scoop

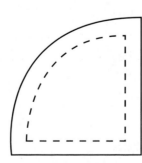

Double-Dip Delight
Small Cone

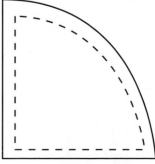

Double-Dip Delight
Large Cone

Spring Flings

Spring is a season of renewal, and also a season of many holidays! Be prepared for every gift-giving occasion with the special projects in this chapter.

Kids will love carrying their Easter eggs in a special Bunny Tote you made just for them. And your mom will adore the Strawberry Fluff Pillow—she'll smile and think of you every time she looks at it! There are gifts to make to decorate the table and gifts for little ones to wear.

So come on—celebrate spring in all its glory (and all its holidays) with these fun-to-sew gifts for those you love!

Bunny Flight Basket

By Chris Malone

Not only a sweet Easter basket, but filled with goodies of any kind this basket makes a great presentation for any spring gift occasion.

Project Specifications

Skill Level: Beginner

Basket Size: Any size

Note: Shop craft stores for basket sales and watch garage sales and thrift shops for bargain baskets.

Materials

- Basket with handle (model is 9" in diameter and 4½" high without handle)
- Approximately ½ yard multicolored pastel print or plaid (amount varies with basket size)
- Scraps of five coordinating colors and green print
- 8" x 12" white knit fabric
- 1 yard 1½"-wide multicolored satin ribbon
- ½ yard 3/8"-wide multicolored satin ribbon
- 5 (⅝"–¾") white buttons
- 1 (1½") white pompom
- 1 (7mm) pink pompom
- 2 (4mm) colored beads for eyes
- 9" white fabric-covered floral wire
- Cardboard to fit bottom of basket
- Batting to fit bottom of basket
- Polyester fiberfill
- Heavy buttonhole or carpet thread
- All-purpose threads to match fabrics
- Hot-glue gun and glue sticks
- Basic sewing supplies and tools

Instructions

Step 1. Measure circumference of basket and multiply by 2½" for length of lining strip. It will probably be necessary to piece two lengths of fabric to obtain the desired length. For width of lining strip measure the depth of the basket and add 3½". For example, the model basket has a circumference of 24" and is 4½" in height. The strip should measure 8" x 60".

Step 2. With right sides of lining strip facing, stitch short ends together forming a tube. Press seam allowance open.

Step 3. Fold one long edge of lining 2" to the wrong side and press. Lightly mark a gathering line with a pencil on wrong side of lining 1½" from the folded top edge and another ½" from bottom raw edge. Place heavy buttonhole or carpet thread over line and stitch over it with a wide zigzag stitch. Backstitch at beginning and end. Do not catch heavy thread in stitches.

Step 4. Pull both ends of heavy thread to gather each line of stitching. Adjust gathers evenly until lining fits inside of basket at top and bottom. Pins will help hold lining against basket while adjusting fit. When fit is correct, tie thread ends to secure.

Step 5. Apply glue to top gathering line, a few inches at a time, and press to inside rim of basket so lining extends 1¼" above top of basket. Apply glue, a few inches at a time, to basket bottom. Pull lining down taut and press gathers to glue.

Step 6. Place basket on cardboard and trace around it. Mark a line ¼"–½" inside of traced line to allow for basket thickness. Cut on inside line. Place cardboard in basket to check fit. Adjust if necessary. Use cardboard as pattern to cut batting. Glue batting to one side of cardboard.

Step 7. Place cardboard on a piece of lining fabric and cut fabric 2" larger all around. Hand-sew a gathering line around fabric ½" from edge. Place cardboard batting side down on wrong side of fabric and pull gathers to bring fabric around edge of cardboard. Knot thread and clip. Apply glue to basket bottom and push cardboard in place, padded fabric side up.

Step 8. For yo-yo flowers, cut one 4¾" circle, two 4" circles and two 3½" circles from coordinating color scraps. Using a matching doubled thread, hand-sew a gathering stitch around the edge of each circle. Pull the gathers tightly to close the center of the circle. Knot, but do not clip thread. Flatten the circle with your fingers and adjust so hole is in the center of the circle. Using same thread, sew a button to the center of each yo-yo over the hole.

Step 9. For leaves, fold green print in half, right sides together. Trace leaf pattern three times on one side of doubled fabric. Sew on traced lines, leaving open at bottom. Cut out close to stitching line and trim point.

Turn right side out and press. Hand-gather along base of each leaf.

Step 10. Tie the wide satin ribbon in a bow with 2½" loops. Tie a knot about 1¾" from end of each streamer; trim ends in a V-cut. Using photo as a guide, arrange bow, flowers and leaves on one side of basket, turning and twisting ribbon streamers and tucking raw edge of leaves under flowers. When satisfied with the arrangement, glue in place.

Step 11. Fold white knit fabric in half and trace rabbit pattern on one side of doubled fabric. Sew all around on traced lines. Do not leave an opening. Cut out ⅛" from seam; clip curves. Cut a slash on one side only where indicated by line on pattern. Turn rabbit right side out through slash. Stuff evenly with polyester fiberfill and close slash with hand stitches. Sew bead to each side of face for eyes, pulling thread gently to indent eye area.

Step 12. Cut fabric-covered floral wire in half and tack the middle of both wires to tip of rabbit nose. Glue the pink pompom over wire centers. Curl wire ends. Glue white pompom to rabbit for tail.

Step 13. Tie ⅜"-wide satin ribbon in a small bow. Tie two knots in each streamer, one near the end and one in the middle. Trim ends in a V-cut. Arrange and glue streamer bow and knots to rabbit as shown. Glue rabbit to front of basket handle. $

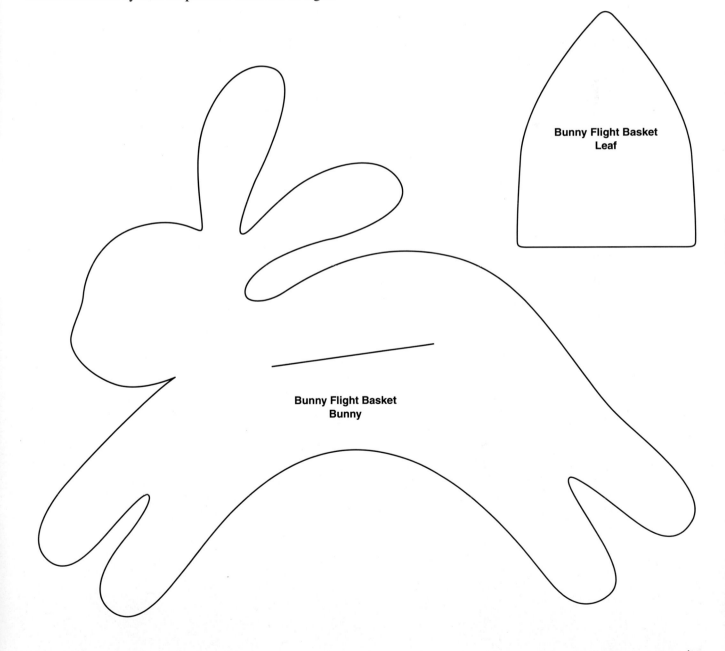

Bunny Flight Basket
Leaf

Bunny Flight Basket
Bunny

Spring Is Sprung Wall Quilt

By Mary Ayres

What could be more appropriate (or economical) to border this more-than-excited little chick than tiny scraps of reproduction feed sacks?

Project Specifications

Skill Level: Beginner

Wall Quilt Size: 12" x 15"

Materials

- 8½" x 11½" white solid for background
- 7½" x 7½" square of yellow print for chick
- Scraps of assorted pastel prints for border, orange for beak and white solid for corners
- Backing fabric 15" x 18"
- Thin cotton batting 15" x 18"
- 4 (¾") white buttons
- Orange, yellow, blue, green and black 6-strand embroidery floss
- 7½" x 7½" fusible transfer web
- 1¾ yards yellow jumbo rickrack
- ¼ yard ⅜"-wide blue-check ribbon
- Yellow feather
- Basic sewing supplies and tools

Instructions

Step 1. Trace chick and beak on paper side of fusible transfer web. Cut out leaving ¼" margin around traced lines. Following manufacturer's instructions, fuse to selected fabrics. Cut out on traced lines.

Step 2. Position chick and beak on white background panel. Head should be 1½" down from top of panel seam line and wing on left side should be ⅞" from seam line. Cut a 2" piece from top of yellow feather. Place ½" of cut end of feather under chick's head at center top. Fuse chick and beak, including feather.

Step 3. Transfer remaining details to center panel. Work buttonhole stitch around outside edge of chick and wing details with 3 strands of yellow embroidery floss. Work buttonhole stitch around beak with 3 strands of orange floss. Embroider stem stitch on legs with 3 strands of orange floss. Embroider words with stem stitch and 2 strands of green floss. Embroider motion lines around chick with 2 strands of blue floss. For eyes, work French knots with 3 strands of black floss wrapped around needle one time for each knot.

Step 4. From pastel prints cut 38 rectangles 1½" x 2½"; cut four white solid squares 2½" x 2½". Sew two sets of 11 pastel rectangles together on long sides and stitch to long sides of center panel. Sew two sets of eight rectangles together on long sides and sew a white square to end of each strip. Sew to top and bottom of center panel.

Step 5. Baste batting to back of quilt front. Sew rickrack around front of quilt ¼" from edge, beginning and ending in a bottom corner, and stitching through the center of the rickrack.

Step 6. Right sides together, sew quilt front to back, leaving a 5" opening along bottom edge. Sew along the previous rickrack stitching. Trim corners and turn right side out. Close opening with hand stitches.

Step 7. Tie blue-check ribbon in a bow and trim ends even. Through all layers, sew center of bow to center of chick's neck.

Step 8. Center a button on each white corner square and sew in place with blue floss, stitching through all layers. $

Beak
Cut 1 orange

**Spring Is Sprung Wall Quilt
Chick**
Cut 1 yellow

Strawberry Fluff Pillow

By June Fiechter

The designer spotted this perfect strawberry fabric
in a thrift-shop dress—a great source of very affordable fabric.

Project Specifications

Skill Level: Beginner

Pillow Size: Approximately 16" x 16" x 4"

Materials

- ¾ yard red print for strawberry
- Ten 5" x 8" scrap pieces of solid green for leaves
- 20 oz. bag of polyester fiberfill
- All-purpose threads to match fabrics
- Fabric glue (optional)
- Basic sewing supplies and tools

Instructions

Step 1. Enlarge patterns, trace and cut fabrics as instructed.

Step 2. Place two green leaf pieces right sides together and stitch around periphery, leaving an opening at one point. Repeat for five leaves.

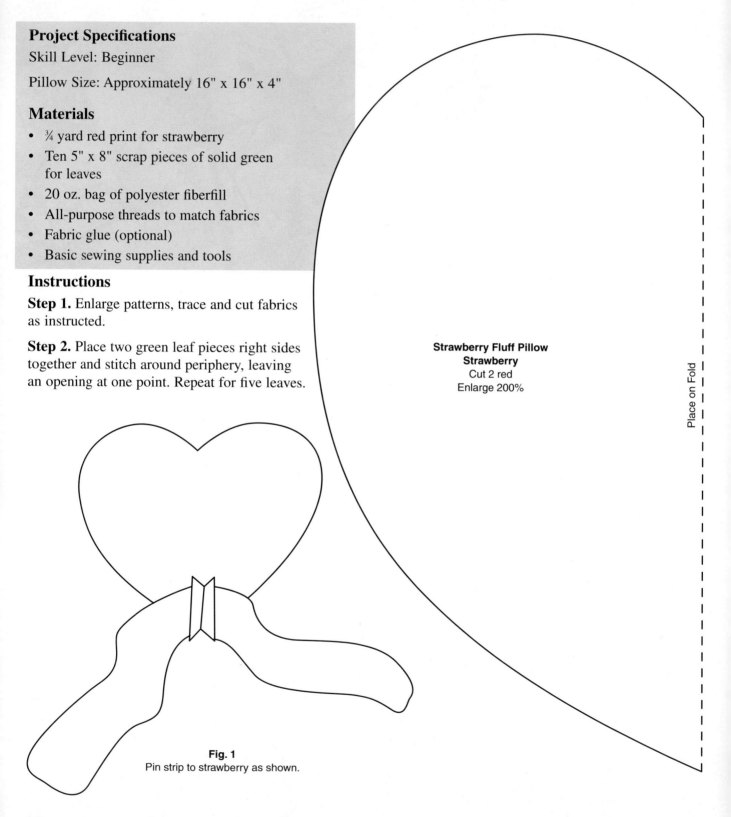

Strawberry Fluff Pillow
Strawberry
Cut 2 red
Enlarge 200%

Place on Fold

Fig. 1
Pin strip to strawberry as shown.

Step 3. Turn leaves right side out. Press and stuff with polyester fiberfill. Stitch a line down the center of the leaf through all thicknesses.

Step 4. From red print cut two strips 4" x 31". Sew together on short ends to make one long strip.

Step 5. Right sides together, match strip seam to bottom front of strawberry as shown in Fig. 1. Continue pinning around strawberry, leaving a 4" opening at the top. Repeat process, pinning other side of strip to back of strawberry. Sew around each side.

Step 6. Turn strawberry right side out and press. Stuff with polyester fiberfill. Insert stuffed leaves in opening and secure with hand stitches or fabric glue. $

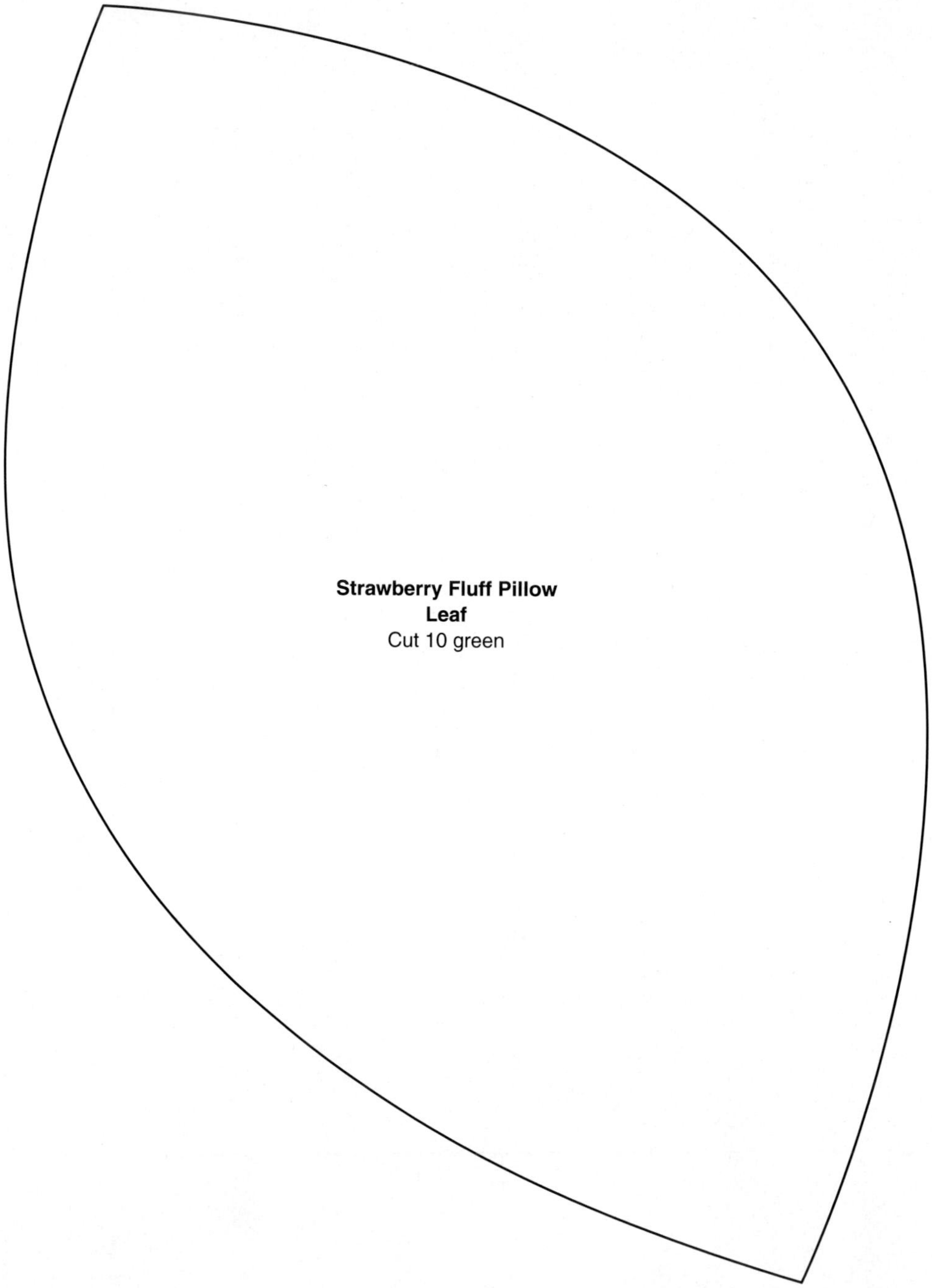

**Strawberry Fluff Pillow
Leaf
Cut 10 green**

Reader's Pillow

By Karen Mead

A search through Granny's linen closet or a quick trip to the thrift shop will probably uncover an appropriate dresser scarf to make this handy accessory.

Project Specifications

Skill Level: Beginner

Pillow Size: Approximately 10½" x 18½"

Materials

- Antique embroidered linen dresser scarf approximately 10" x 16"
- 22" piece of ½"-wide satin ribbon to match dresser scarf design
- ⅜ yard coordinating print fabric
- Cardboard 10½" x 18½"
- All-purpose thread to match fabrics
- Polyester fiberfill
- Basic sewing supplies and tools

Instructions

Step 1. From print fabric cut one piece 13" x 21" and another 11" x 19".

Step 2. Center and stitch the dresser scarf directly to the 13" x 21" piece of fabric to make pillow top.

Step 3. Make ½" darts at the corners of the pillow top as shown in Fig. 1.

Step 4. Cut ribbon into 9" and 13" lengths. On right side of pillow top, pin both ribbons at center of one long side. Place the longer ribbon first with the shorter piece on top. Both ribbons should be right side up. Pin in place.

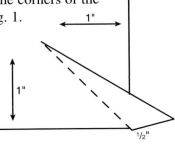

Fig. 1
Make ½" darts at corners as shown.

Step 5. With right sides facing, pin the two fabric pieces right sides together. Stitch around periphery leaving one 11" end open. Both ends of the 13" ribbon should be stitched in the seams. Only one end of the 9" ribbon will be stitched in a seam.

Step 6. Clip corners and turn right side out. Slip cardboard into pillow creating a hard surface for pillow

Continued on page 50

Teatime Pot Holders

By June Fiechter

Somehow Alice in Wonderland *comes to mind at the sight of these tea-party-perfect hot pads.*

Project Specifications

Skill Level: Beginner

Pot Holder Size: 8" x 8½"

Materials

- 4 pieces blue-and-white check 8" x 8½"
- ¼ yard yellow with pink flowers for bottom cup, teapot trim and binding
- Scraps of blue-green-white plaid, pink plaid, pink floral, green leaf print, and white with pink print
- ⅛ yard fusible transfer web
- 4 pieces cotton batting 8" x 8½"
- Black and white all-purpose thread
- Basic sewing supplies and tools

Instructions

Step 1. Trace appliqué patterns on paper side of fusible transfer web. Cut out, leaving roughly ¼" margin around traced lines. Following manufacturer's instructions, fuse to selected fabrics and cut out on traced lines.

Step 2. Referring to photo for placement, arrange appliqué pieces on two blue-and-white-check background pieces. Fuse in place. Machine-appliqué around all pieces with white thread and narrow zigzag stitch.

Step 3. Referring to photo, draw handle on kettle. With white thread, satin-stitch handle.

Step 4. The remaining two blue-and-white-check pieces are for backing. Layer two pieces of batting between appliquéd pieces and backing pieces for each pot holder. Pin in place.

Step 5. With white thread, machine-quilt horizontal lines at approximately 1¼" intervals across each hot pad. Do not stitch across appliqué pieces, but do stitch a quilting line around the designs.

Step 6. With black thread, outline all design pieces for detailing.

Step 7. Using the yellow with pink flowers fabric, make 2¼ yards of 2½"-wide bias binding. Press in half lengthwise with wrong sides together. Bind each pot holder, starting at upper left corner. When returning to starting point, create a hanging loop before finishing off. $

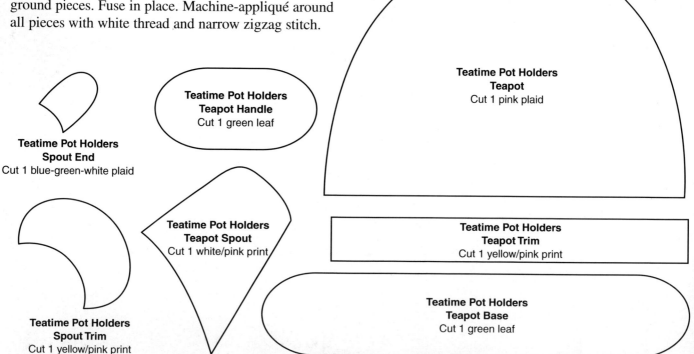

Teatime Pot Holders Spout End
Cut 1 blue-green-white plaid

Teatime Pot Holders Teapot Handle
Cut 1 green leaf

Teatime Pot Holders Teapot
Cut 1 pink plaid

Teatime Pot Holders Teapot Spout
Cut 1 white/pink print

Teatime Pot Holders Teapot Trim
Cut 1 yellow/pink print

Teatime Pot Holders Spout Trim
Cut 1 yellow/pink print

Teatime Pot Holders Teapot Base
Cut 1 green leaf

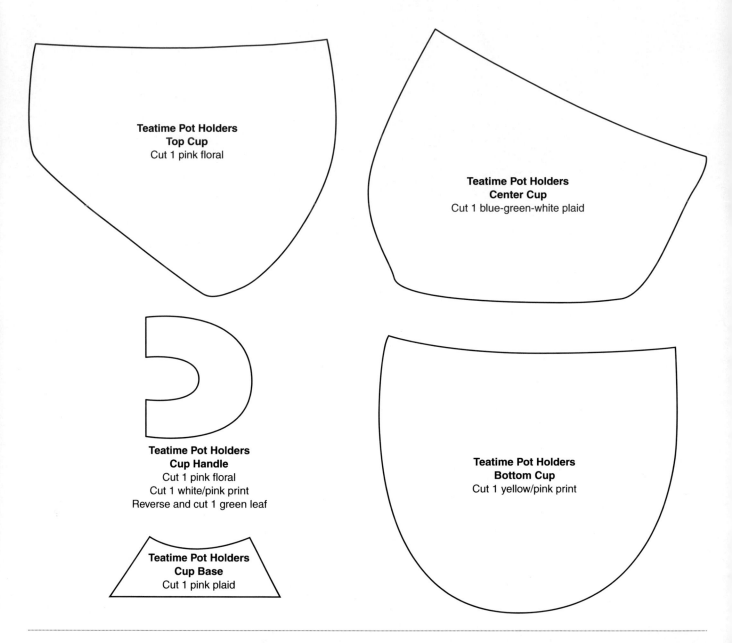

Teatime Pot Holders
Top Cup
Cut 1 pink floral

Teatime Pot Holders
Center Cup
Cut 1 blue-green-white plaid

Teatime Pot Holders
Cup Handle
Cut 1 pink floral
Cut 1 white/pink print
Reverse and cut 1 green leaf

Teatime Pot Holders
Bottom Cup
Cut 1 yellow/pink print

Teatime Pot Holders
Cup Base
Cut 1 pink plaid

Reader's Pillow

Continued from page 47

bottom. Stuff top side of pillow, filling out dart corners and evenly stuffing all the surface of pillow.

Step 7. Fold in the raw edges of the open end and close with hand stitches. $

Bunny Tote

By Marian Shenk

*Big enough to carry all the essentials, but small and cute enough
for little girls to carry treasures from place to place.*

Project Specifications

Skill Level: Beginner

Tote Bag Size: Approximately 8" x 3" x 9¾"

Materials

- ¾ yard beige print for bag and lining
- ⅓ yard soft interfacing
- Scraps of orange, green, lavender and pink for appliqué
- 6" x 10" white fleece for bunny
- 3 (½") purple buttons
- 8" (⅛"-wide) purple satin ribbon
- 16" (⅛"-wide) green satin ribbon
- Dark gray 6-strand embroidery floss
- Firm cardboard 3" x 8"
- Fabric glue
- All-purpose threads to match fabrics
- Clear nylon monofilament
- Small amount of polyester fiberfill
- Basic sewing supplies and tools

Instructions

Step 1. From beige print cut one piece 12" x 28" for bag and one piece 12" x 22½" for lining.

Step 2. From interfacing cut one piece 12" x 22½". Center interfacing on wrong side of bag fabric. Fold extra fabric at top down over interfacing and press.

Step 3. Trace and cut bunny and ears as directed on pattern. Center bunny 1" from top edge on front right side of bag piece as shown in Fig. 1, With clear nylon monofilament, machine-appliqué

12"

1"

Fig. 1
Center bunny on bag as shown.

bunny in place. Appliqué inner ear pieces in place.

Step 4. From lavender scrap cut a piece 5" x 9" for dress. Fold in half, right sides together, to make a 4½" x 5" piece; sew the two side edges together. Turn right side out and press. Gather across the top raw edge to fit neck of bunny and baste. Zigzag a piece of ⅛"-wide purple satin ribbon over the raw gathered edge.

Step 5. Referring to photo throughout, place dress over bunny. Tack sides of dress in place and sew three purple buttons down front. Make a small bow from ⅛"-wide purple satin ribbon and tack in place.

Step 6. With 2 strands of gray embroidery floss, embroider face details and whiskers.

Step 7. Trace and cut carrots as directed on pattern. For carrot tops cut two pieces 2" x 5" from green scraps.

Step 8. With right sides together sew from point to top of carrot. Turn right side out. Fold top raw edge under ¼" and run a gathering stitch around the opening. Stuff with fiberfill. Repeat for two carrots.

Step 9. Fold green tops in half, short end to short end, and insert the fold into the open top of the carrot. Draw up gathers tightly and sew to top of carrot. Snip green tops from open end to stitching at ¼" intervals to make loose leaves. Cut two 8" pieces of ⅛"-wide green satin ribbon and tie a tiny bow around each carrot top.

Step 10. Refer to photo for placement of carrots and hand-sew to secure.

Step 11. Fold right sides of bag together and sew the side seams. Repeat for lining. Turn bag right side out and insert lining inside bag, fastening the top under the previously folded-down edge. Hand-stitch in place.

Step 12. From beige print cut two strips 3½" x 17" for handles. Fold each in half lengthwise, right sides together, and sew. Turn right side out. Press ends under to form points as shown in Fig. 2.

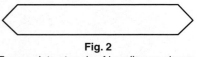

Fig. 2
Form points at ends of handles as shown.

Step 13. Pin handles about 2" from side seams and topstitch in place.

Step 14. From beige print cut one piece 6" x 11". Center cardboard on fabric. Wrap sides and corners neatly and glue to secure. When glue has dried, place in bottom of bag. Fold in corners at bottom of bag to form gusset. Remove cardboard and stitch across fold of bag. Glue fabric-covered cardboard in bottom of bag to finish. $

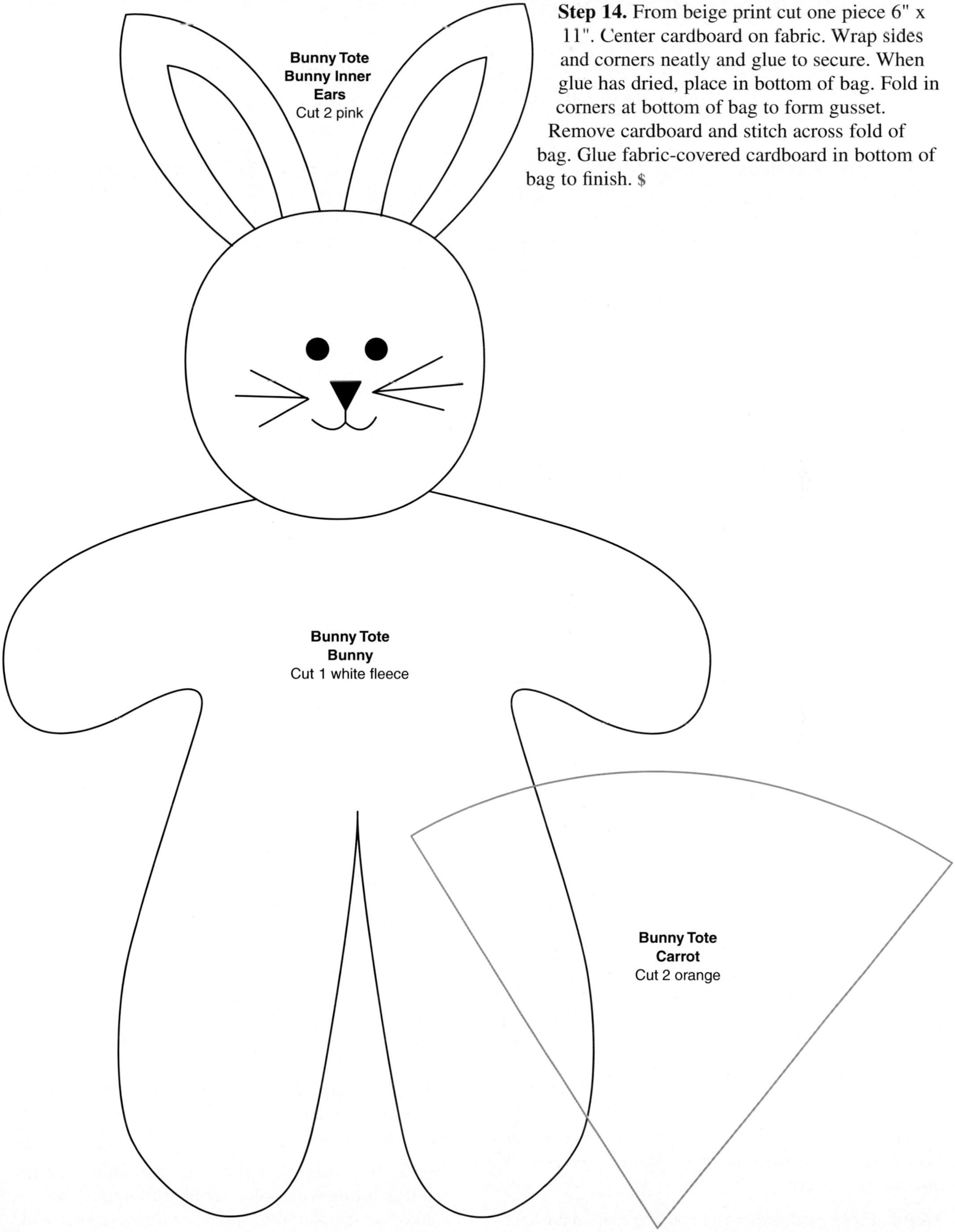
Bunny Tote
Bunny Inner Ears
Cut 2 pink
Bunny Tote
Bunny
Cut 1 white fleece
Bunny Tote
Carrot
Cut 2 orange

Dolly & Me Jumpers

By Judith Sandstrom

Make this adorable soft doll for a special little girl and dress them both in matching fresh spring outfits.

Project Specifications

Skill Level: Beginner

Dress Size: Any size

Doll Size: 14"

Note: Child's dress was made in size 5 and required 1 yard of 60" fabric. This yardage included enough for doll jumper, also.

Materials

- McCalls pattern 2822
- Fabric as specified on pattern plus ¼ yard for doll jumper
- Facing and interfacing fabric as specified on pattern
- ¼ yard lining fabric for doll jumper
- ¼ yard muslin for doll
- Scraps of pink, blue, lavender, yellow, rose and light green for yo-yos
- Scraps of white fabric for doll bloomers and blouse
- 1 package curly hair
- Polyester fiberfill
- Water-soluble marker
- Brown and rose 6-strand embroidery floss
- 24" (⅛"-wide) elastic
- Plastic or cardboard template material
- 2 snaps or hook-and-loop tape scraps
- 1 package emerald green jumbo rickrack
- 1 package emerald green baby rickrack
- All-purpose threads to match fabrics and rickrack
- Basic sewing supplies and tools

Instructions

Child's Jumper

Note: *Seam allowances for child's jumper are ⅝". All other seam allowances are ¼".*

Step 1. Cut out jumper, facings and interfacings as directed on pattern.

Step 2. From cardboard or plastic template material make a circle template 3¼" in diameter. Trace around circle once on each of the six fabric scrap colors. Cut out on traced lines. Fold under ¼" at the edge of the circle. Using double strand of matching color thread, hand-gather close to the folded edge. Pull stitches tightly and knot thread. Do not cut thread.

Step 3. Cut circle template in half. With water-soluble marker, trace scallops 3½" from lower edge of jumper front as shown in Fig. 1.

Fig. 1
Trace scallops on jumper as shown.

Step 4. Center emerald green jumbo rickrack on traced line and stitch by hand or machine.

Step 5. Follow pattern directions to stitch and hem jumper.

Step 6. Using remaining thread on each yo-yo, stitch one yo-yo to top peak of each rickrack scallop.

Doll

Step 1. Trace doll pattern pieces on doubled muslin leaving ½" between pieces. Trace arm and leg patterns twice, body once. Stitch around pieces through both layers of muslin, leaving ends open for stuffing. Cut out ⅛" outside traced line.

Step 2. Turn each piece right side out. Stuff the arms and legs firmly with polyester fiberfill to the lines marked on the patterns. Stitch across these knee and

elbow lines, then stuff the remainder of the limbs more loosely.

Step 3. Baste across top of legs at raw edges. Turn in the raw edges of the arms and close opening with hand stitches.

Step 4. Firmly stuff head and upper body. Right sides together and raw edges aligned, pin legs to front of body. Stitch, making sure not to catch back of body. Finish stuffing body, turn in back edge and close opening with hand stitches.

Step 5. Hand-stitch arms to side seam line with top of arm at shoulder. Thumbs should point upward.

Step 6. Following manufacturer's instructions, sew or glue hair to preferred length and style.

Step 7. Transfer eye and mouth markings to face. Embroider eyes with 1 strand of brown embroidery floss and mouth with 1 strand of rose.

Doll Jumper

Step 1. Trace and cut jumper pieces as directed on pattern.

Step 2. Press under ¼" seam allowance on sides and shoulder seams of both lining pieces.

Step 3. From cardboard or plastic template material make a circle template 2" in diameter. Trace around circle once on four different fabric scraps. Cut out on traced lines. Fold under ³⁄₁₆" at the edge of the circle. Using double strand of matching color thread, hand-gather close to the folded edge. Pull stitches tightly and knot thread. Do not cut thread.

Step 4. Cut circle template in half. With water-soluble marker, trace scallops 1¼" from lower edge of jumper front as in Child's Jumper, Step 3.

Step 5. Center emerald green baby rickrack on traced line and stitch by hand or machine.

Step 6. With right sides together, pin each jumper piece to a lining piece. Stitch around the neckline, armhole and bottom edge, stopping at the edge of the lining. Reinforce and clip curves. Turn right side out and press.

Step 7. With right sides together, stitch the jumper front to the jumper back at the shoulder edges and sides, taking care not to catch the lining in the stitching. Tuck the jumper edges into the lining and slip-stitch the lining edges together.

Step 8. Stitch each yo-yo to peaks of rickrack scallops.

Doll Blouse

Step 1. From white scraps cut blouse as directed on pattern.

Step 2. Turn back edges under twice and stitch to hem.

Step 3. Stitch front to back at shoulder seams.

Step 4. Turn neck edge under and stitch. Pull thread to gather slightly and knot on wrong side.

Step 5. Turn under twice and stitch a casing on both sleeve edges. Insert a 3½" piece of elastic in each sleeve and stitch across ends.

Step 6. Stitch a continuous underarm and side seam. Reinforce and clip at underarm.

Step 7. Turn bottom hem under twice and stitch.

Step 8. Attach snaps or hook-and-loop tape to fasten back.

Doll Bloomers

Step 1. From white scraps cut bloomers as directed on pattern.

Step 2. Turn lower edges under twice and stitch to form casing.

Step 3. Insert a 4" piece of elastic in each piece and stitch across ends.

Step 4. Stitch one side to the other in front and in back. Stitch one continuous underleg seam, matching the front and back seams.

Step 5. Turn waist under twice and stitch to form casing, leaving a 1" opening at back seam. Insert 8" piece of elastic and stitch the ends. Finish stitching casing closed. $

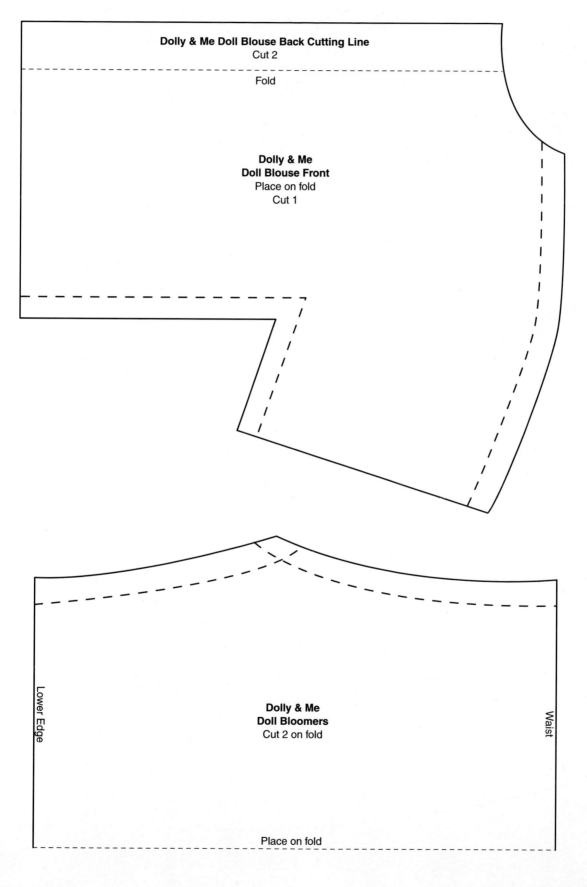

Dolly & Me Doll Blouse Back Cutting Line
Cut 2

Fold

**Dolly & Me
Doll Blouse Front**
Place on fold
Cut 1

Lower Edge

**Dolly & Me
Doll Bloomers**
Cut 2 on fold

Waist

Place on fold

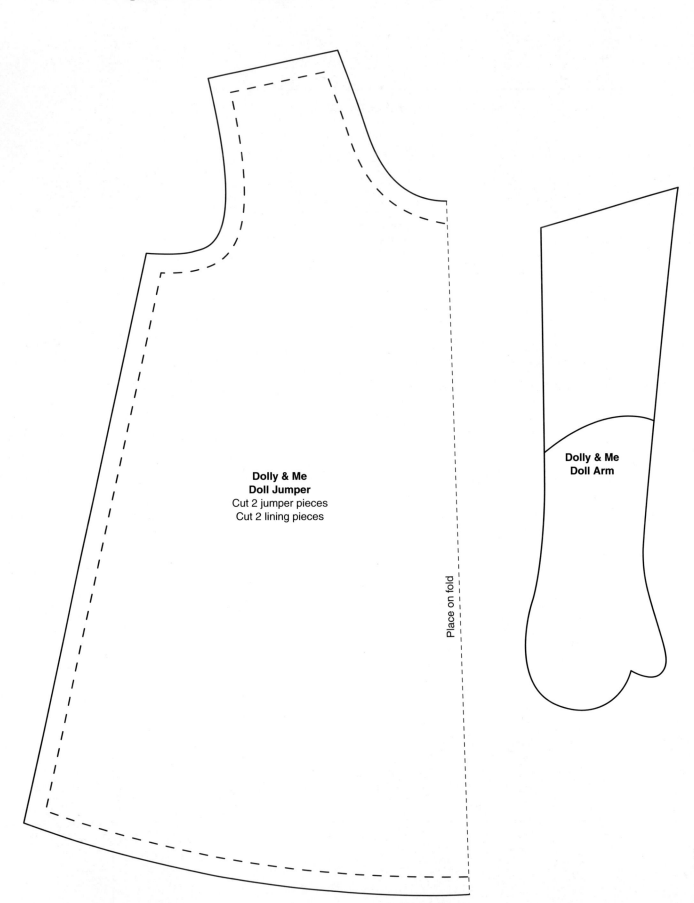

**Dolly & Me
Doll Jumper**
Cut 2 jumper pieces
Cut 2 lining pieces

Place on fold

**Dolly & Me
Doll Arm**

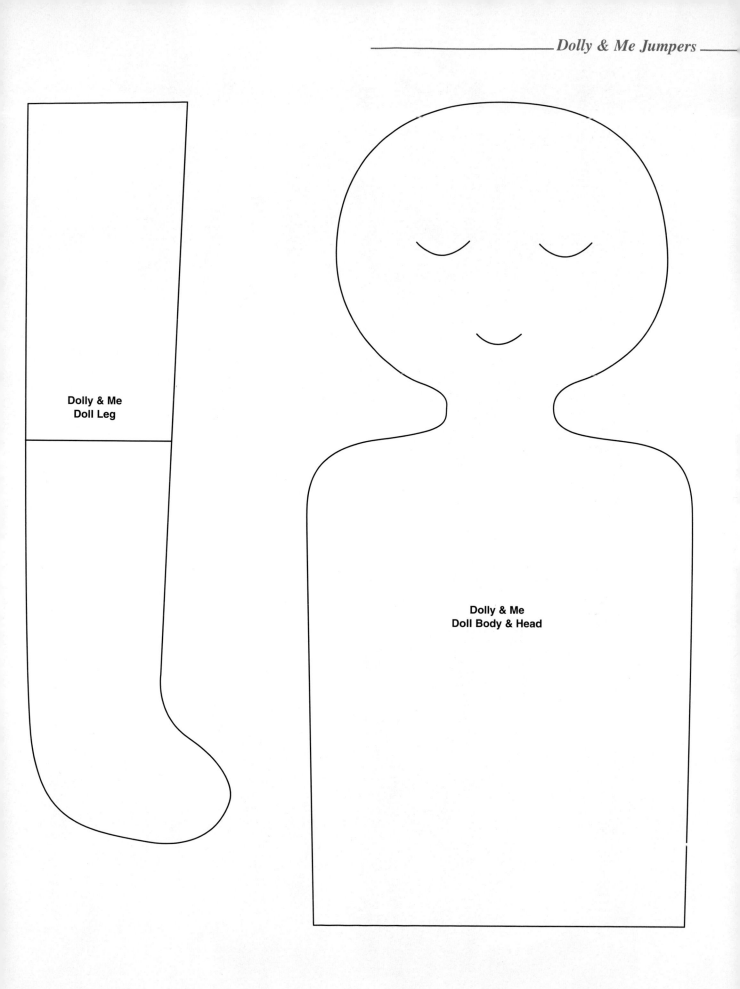

Dolly & Me
Doll Leg

Dolly & Me
Doll Body & Head

Summer Celebrations

Summer is a time of picnics, gardening and holidays!

We all know people who spend warm summer days in their vegetable or flower gardens. Show them you appreciate their work with a garden hat to help keep them cool when the sun is high in the sky. Stitch a fanciful fish place mat and napkin ring set just in time for Dad and Father's Day. And what little girl wouldn't love to wear the Sweet Little Ladybug Dress Set to summer tea parties?

Whether you enjoy staying inside in the cool air conditioning to work on your projects or whether you bask in the sun as you hand-sew buttons to decorate a pillow, enjoy these fun-to-stitch projects!

Smocked Gingham Garden Hat

By Donna Friebertshauser

Make your cover-up protection from sunburn both attractive and fun with this clever design.

Project Specifications

Skill Level: Beginner

Hat Size: Any size

Materials

- 1 yard gingham with 1" squares
- All-purpose thread to match gingham
- Beeswax (optional)
- Water-soluble pen
- Basic sewing supplies and tools

Instructions

Smocking

Step 1. Count out a length of gingham that includes 34 complete squares. Add ¼" to each end for seam allowance. Count out 28 full squares in the other direction. Cut fabric to that size.

Step 2. Bring right sides of short ends together and sew a ¼" seam. Press seam open.

Step 3. Fold under ½" twice on one raw edge of cylinder and hem, leaving a full 27 squares for hat and brim.

Step 4. Smocking is worked around the wrong side of cylinder. With the water-soluble pen make a dot on the upper left corner of each square of the seventh row from hemmed end of cylinder. Mark the ninth, eleventh, thirteenth and fifteenth rows in the same manner.

Step 5. One row of smocking requires two squares of gingham. The five marked rows are the centers of five rows of smocking for a total of 10 squares of gingham.

Step 6. The smocking stitch is a small, horizontal stitch taken at the corner of each indicated square. A single or double length of thread may be used, but do not work with a long thread because it tangles. Running your sewing thread through beeswax will make stitching easier.

Step 7. Begin smocking at any marked dot on the seventh row and stitch around the cylinder. Follow needle-movement numbers as shown in Fig. 1.

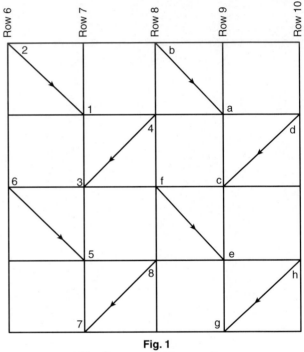

Fig. 1
Needle movement for smocking.

Step 8. Take a small horizontal stitch at the lower corner of the first square (1). Take a second small stitch in the same place to firmly anchor the thread in the fabric.

Step 9. Take a small stitch at the upper right corner of that same square (2) and pull to meet (1). Sew the two corners together with several small stitches.

Step 10. Move down row 7 to the bottom of the next square (3). Take the small horizontal stitch. The thread from (2/1) will be on the surface of the fabric. Pass the needle behind that thread and through the loop to knot the thread. It is extremely important to knot this stitch before proceeding with more smocking.

Step 11. Move to the upper right corner of row 8 (4). Take the horizontal stitch and pull the corner back to the central line of row 7. Securely sew the corners together.

Step 12. Continue in this manner until one row of smocking has been stitched around the cylinder.

Step 13. Work a second row of smocking using row 9
Continued on page 66

Sweet Little Ladybug Dress Set

By June Feichter

*Buy a little dress and white socks and the other two pieces of this set
can be recycled from your own stash or thrift-shop treasures.*

Project Specifications

Skill Level: Beginner

Dress and Sock Size: Any size

Barrette Size: 4½" x 2¼"

Purse Size: Approximately 7½" x 9"

Materials

- Purchased red dress with dropped waistline
- Scraps of green for leaves
- ½ yard light blue denim or recycled denim
- 1¼ yards ¼"-wide black fusible bias tape
- 8" (1"-wide) red-and-white polka-dot grosgrain ribbon
- 10 (¼") black buttons for ladybug spots
- 2 (⅜") black buttons for ladybug eyes
- 2 (¾") red shank buttons for purse
- 2 (½") red buttons for socks
- 1 (½") black button for barrette
- Scraps of paper-backed fusible transfer web
- ⅔ yard non-paper-backed fusible web
- 3" barrette clasp
- Black 6-strand embroidery floss
- 30" red cord or recycled sweatshirt string
- All-purpose threads to match fabrics
- Hot-glue gun and glue
- Basic sewing supplies and tools

Instructions

Dress

Step 1. Draw a circle 7" in diameter on center front of dress. Press fusible bias tape over circle. Referring to photo, cut another strip of fusible bias tape for head and one for a line down center back. Press to fuse in place.

Step 2. Trace leaf shapes on paper side of fusible transfer web as directed on pattern. Cut out, leaving roughly ¼" margin around traced lines.

Step 3. Following manufacturer's instructions, fuse leaves to selected fabrics. Cut out on traced lines. Referring to photo, arrange around ladybug and fuse in place. With black all-purpose thread, zigzag around leaves.

Step 4. With black all-purpose thread and straight stitch, sew along each edge of bias tape.

Step 5. Draw two circles 1" in diameter on paper side of fusible transfer web. Cut and fuse to blue denim as in Steps 2 and 3 above. Referring to photo, place eyes on ladybug face and fuse. With 6 strands of black embroidery floss, outline eye circles.

Step 6. Referring to photo for placement, sew appropriate buttons on ladybug back and on eyes.

Step 7. Make couching for antenna and leaf veins by laying 6 strands of black embroidery floss on drawn lines and working a machine zigzag stitch over floss to secure in place.

Barrette

Step 1. From blue denim fabric cut bow as directed on pattern. Right sides together, stitch all the way around periphery. Cut a small slit on back of bow and turn right side out through slit. Close opening with hand stitches.

Step 2. From blue denim fabric cut a strip 1" x 1¼". Fold two longer edges to center and press. Wrap strip around center of bow and overlap ends to gather center of bow. Secure with basting stitches.

Step 3. Following manufacturer's instructions, fuse non-paper-backed fusible web between two green fabric scraps 1½" x 2½". Trace and cut two leaves.

Step 4. Tie bow with red-and-white polka-dot grosgrain ribbon. Glue ½" black button to center of bow. Glue leaves to top of denim bow. Glue polka-dot bow to denim bow, on top of leaves.

Step 5. Glue barrette clasp to back of denim bow.

Socks

Step 1. Cut two blue denim strips 2" x 12". Fold in

half lengthwise, right sides together, and zigzag to cuff of sock. Stretch the sock as you sew, but not the denim. Repeat with second sock.

Step 2. Cut two 3" strips of ¼"-wide black fusible bias tape. Bring two ends of one piece together at center and press to hold bow shape. Repeat with second strip.

Step 3. Sew bias bow to outside of each cuff. Sew one ½" red button to center of each black bias bow.

Purse

Step 1. From blue denim cut two pieces 8" x 23". Place two pieces together and draw a half-circle curve at one end as shown in Fig. 1. Cut along curve.

Step 2. Cut one piece of non-paper-backed fusible web ¼" smaller all around than pieces cut in Step 1. Following manufacturer's instructions, center and bond to wrong side of one piece of denim.

Step 3. Trace leaves on paper side of fusible transfer web as directed on pattern. Cut out, leaving approximately ¼" margin around traced lines. Fuse to selected fabrics and cut out on traced lines.

Step 4. Referring to photo for placement, position leaves on curved end of interfaced denim and fuse. With black thread, machine-zigzag around leaves.

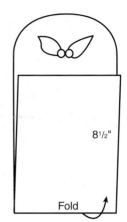
Fig. 1
Draw curve at one end of denim strips as shown.

Make couching for leaf veins by laying 6 strands of black embroidery floss down center of leaf and working machine zigzag stitch over floss to secure in place.

Step 5. Sew ¾" red shank buttons in place between leaves.

Step 6. Right sides together, fold straight end of piece up 8½" as shown in Fig 2. Stitch sides together with ¼" seam. Repeat with other denim piece.

Step 7. With right sides together, sew the half-circle edges of both denim pieces together and turn right side out as shown in Fig. 3. Push lining down inside purse.

Step 8. Fold edges of remaining ends under and topstitch, catching ends of 30" red cord at each end.

Step 9. Smooth all fabric and press to activate bonding action of fusible web. $

8½"
Fold
Fig. 2
Fold straight end up as shown.

Fig. 3
Sew curved ends of denim together as shown.

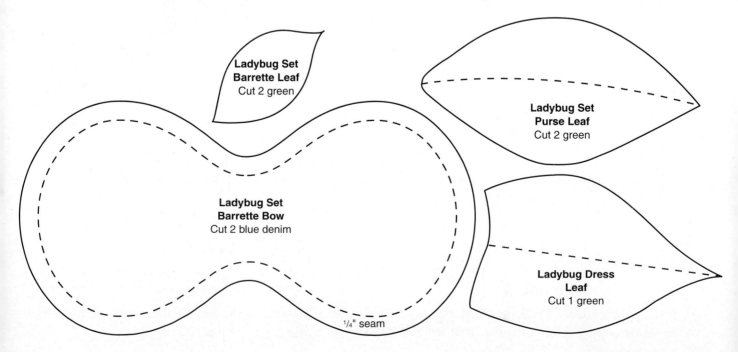

Ladybug Set Barrette Leaf Cut 2 green

Ladybug Set Purse Leaf Cut 2 green

Ladybug Set Barrette Bow Cut 2 blue denim

Ladybug Dress Leaf Cut 1 green

¼" seam

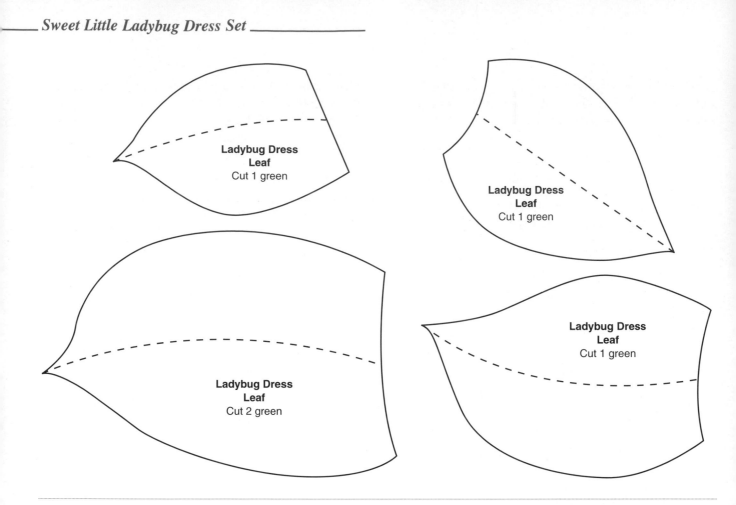

Ladybug Dress
Leaf
Cut 1 green

Ladybug Dress
Leaf
Cut 1 green

Ladybug Dress
Leaf
Cut 2 green

Ladybug Dress
Leaf
Cut 1 green

Smocked Gingham Garden Hat

Continued from page 62

as the center line with the appropriate corners pulled to the center: b to a, stitch together; a to c, knot the stitch; d to c, stitch together; c to e and knot the stitch. Fig. 2 shows the appearance of the smocking on the wrong side facing you.

Step 14. Work three more smocked rows in the same manner. This will be center rows 11, 13 and 15 for a total of five rows of smocking.

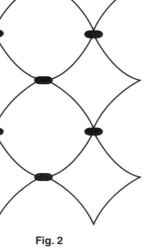

Fig. 2
View of first two smocked rows from wrong side.

Crown

Step 1. Turn the hat right side out. Fold three squares to the inside (wrong side) of the hat. That will leave

three squares of plain fabric before the smocked rows. The three rows of squares inside the crown will help retain the shape of the hat.

Step 2. Pick up a top corner of a square and place it on the corresponding corner of the same colored square. Stitch together. Continue in this manner around the entire cylinder to close the crown. Keep the center hole as small as possible.

Brim

Step 1. Leave three squares of gingham beyond the last row of smocking for a 3" brim. Fold the remaining fabric back on itself toward the last smocked row. Sew the underside of the brim to the last row of smocking.

Step 2. Immerse the entire hat in cold water to remove the marked dots. Dry and enjoy! $

Homespun Charm Kitchen Towels

By Julie Weaver

Ready-made towels can be purchased very inexpensively. Add fabric scraps and a bit of time and imagination for a charming and thoughtful "I made it myself" gift.

Project Specifications

Skill Level: Beginner

Towel Size: Approximately 20" x 28"

Materials

- 2 purchased homespun towels 20" x 28"
- Dark and light gold, green, brown and rust scraps for appliqué
- ¼ yard fusible transfer web
- Threads to match scraps for machine-appliqué
- Basic sewing supplies and tools

Instructions

Step 1. Trace appliqué shapes on paper side of fusible transfer web. Cut out, leaving approximately ¼" margin around traced lines.

Step 2. Following manufacturer's directions, fuse shapes to selected fabrics. Cut out on traced lines.

Step 3. Arrange shapes on bottom left quadrant of each towel, referring to photo for placement. Fuse in place.

Step 4. With matching threads, satin-stitch around all shapes to finish edges. $

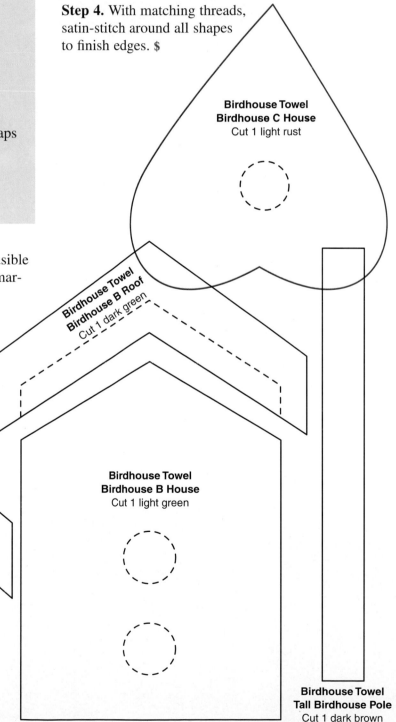

Birdhouse Towel
Birdhouse C House
Cut 1 light rust

Birdhouse Towel
Birdhouse B Roof
Cut 1 dark green

Birdhouse Towel
Birdhouse B House
Cut 1 light green

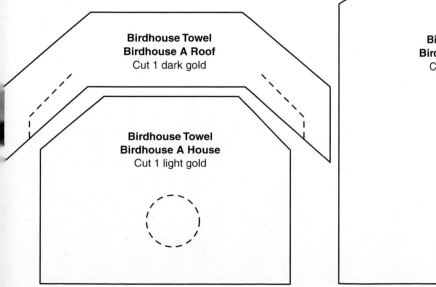

Birdhouse Towel
Birdhouse A Roof
Cut 1 dark gold

Birdhouse Towel
Birdhouse A House
Cut 1 light gold

Birdhouse Towel
Tall Birdhouse Pole
Cut 1 dark brown

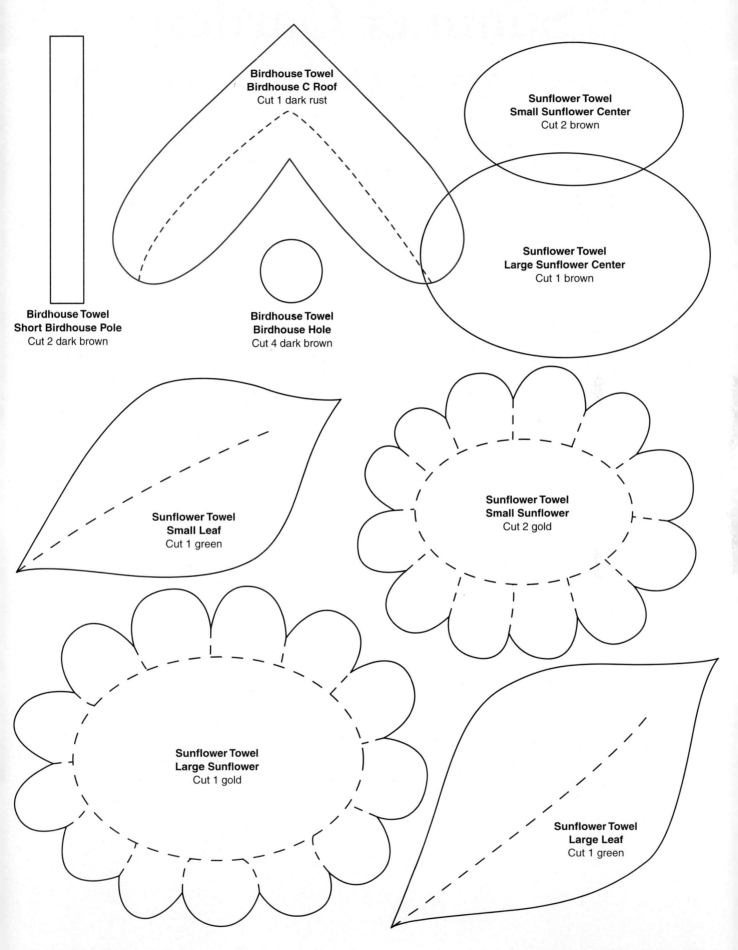

Birdhouse Towel
Birdhouse C Roof
Cut 1 dark rust

Sunflower Towel
Small Sunflower Center
Cut 2 brown

Sunflower Towel
Large Sunflower Center
Cut 1 brown

Birdhouse Towel
Short Birdhouse Pole
Cut 2 dark brown

Birdhouse Towel
Birdhouse Hole
Cut 4 dark brown

Sunflower Towel
Small Leaf
Cut 1 green

Sunflower Towel
Small Sunflower
Cut 2 gold

Sunflower Towel
Large Sunflower
Cut 1 gold

Sunflower Towel
Large Leaf
Cut 1 green

Summer Garden Snack Trays & Coaster Set

By Marian Shenk

*Start with a preprinted pillow panel and quickly
and easily transform the parts into a wonderful hostess gift set.*

Project Specifications

Skill Level: Beginner

Tray Size: Varies with panel size

Coaster Size: 3¾" x 3¾"

Materials

- 1 preprinted pillow panel
- ½ yard coordinating fabric for lining
- 1 piece of foam board
- Coordinating purchased bias tape or scraps from previous projects
- 4 pieces of batting 4¼" x 4¼"
- All-purpose thread to match fabrics
- Basic sewing supplies and tools

Instructions

Snack Tray

Step 1. Cut out pillow panel adding ¼" to each side for seam allowance.

Step 2. Stitch close to edges of bias tape to close opening. Cut into eight 7" lengths. Pin one length 2" each side of each corner of panel, raw edges aligned.

Step 3. Cut a square of lining fabric the same size as pillow panel. Place on top of panel and sew pieces together around three sides, catching the pinned ties in the seams.

Step 4. Cut a piece of foam board the same size as the top border of the panel less 2" on each end for corners; slip between panel and lining. With zipper foot, stitch close to edge of board to hold in place. Continue to stitch on the border line, through panel and lining layers,
along the two sides of panel. Do not sew lower border.

Step 5. Cut a piece of foam board the same size as the center design square and slip between both fabric layers. Machine-stitch along bottom of square to hold board in place.

Step 6. Cut two pieces of foam board the size of the side borders and slide between fabric layers. Cut another piece of foam board for the lower border and slide between fabrics. Close the open seam at bottom with hand stitches.

Step 7. Tie corners together to form sides of tray.

Coasters

Step 1. Pillow panels usually have several design elements. Select appropriate portions and cut four squares 4¼" x 4¼". Place each on top of a batting square.

Step 2. From lining fabric cut four pieces 4½" x 4¼". Wrong sides together, bring the 4¼" ends of each together and press. Place each folded piece on top of design square, raw edges aligned with top raw edge of design square.

Step 3. From lining fabric cut four pieces 3¼" x 4¼". Turn ¼" under along one 4¼" edge, press and stitch. Place each face down on a design square, aligning raw 4¼" edge with lower edge of design square. The hemmed edge will overlap the folded edge.

Step 4. Stitch around all four sides through all layers. Trim corners and seams. Turn right side out through overlap. Poke out corners and press.

Note: Depending on the purchased panel, there still may be enough fabric for a smaller tray. Follow the same snack tray directions, adjusting sizes as necessary. $

Fanciful Fish
Place Mat & Napkin Ring

By Mary Ayres

Summer translates "fishing" to anglers and this set is perfect for serving up the prize catch!

Project Specifications

Skill Level: Beginner

Place Mat Size: 17" x 12"

Napkin Size: 16" x 16"

Note: Materials are for one place mat, one napkin and one napkin ring.

Materials

- ⅜ yard navy print for center panel, corners and backing
- Scraps of gray solid and gray print for fish
- 17" x 17" square of gray solid for napkin
- Scraps of 6 different purple prints for borders and fish tail and fins
- 1 (½") gray button with 2 holes for eye
- Gray pearl cotton
- 2¼ yards navy blue piping
- Scraps of fusible transfer web
- Thin cotton batting 17½" x 12½" and 1½" x 8½"
- Basic sewing supplies and tools

Instructions

Place Mat

Step 1. From navy print cut center panel 11½" x 6½" and four corner squares 3½" x 3½".

Step 2. From one purple print cut eight rectangles 1½" x 3½" for ends of four border sections. From another purple print cut two rectangles 1½" x 3½" for center sections of top and bottom borders. From the remaining four purple prints cut six rectangles each 1½" x 3½".

Step 3. Referring to the photo for placement, sew two identical sets of eleven print rectangles. Order should be mirror image each side of center section. Sew strips to top and bottom of center panel.

Step 4. Referring to photo, sew two identical sets of six print rectangles together for side borders. Add a navy print corner square to each end. Reverse color order of each strip and sew to sides of center panel.

Step 5. Trace fish appliqué pieces on paper side of fusible transfer web. Cut out pieces leaving approximately ¼" margin around each piece. Fuse to selected fabrics following manufacturer's instructions. Select a different purple fabric for each fin and tail. Cut out on traced lines.

Step 6. Position pieces on center panel and fuse.

Step 7. With gray pearl cotton, work buttonhole stitch around all pieces. Sew button at an angle with pearl cotton as indicated on pattern for eye.

Step 8. Baste batting to backside of front. Sew piping around front ¼" from edge, beginning and ending in a bottom corner. Clip piping seams at corners.

Step 9. From navy print cut a backing piece the same size as front. Right sides facing, sew front to back leaving a 5" opening along bottom. Sew directly on piping stitching line. Trim corners and turn right side out. Close opening with hand stitches.

Napkin Ring & Napkin

Step 1. From same purple print used for centers of top and bottom borders of place mat, cut two strips 1½" x 8½". Baste same-size batting strip to back of one fabric strip, which will be the front of the napkin ring.

Step 2. Sew piping to both long edges of front ¼" from edge.

Step 3. Right sides together, sew front to back leaving short ends open. Sew directly on piping stitching line.

Step 4. Turn strip right side out. Sew short front sides together forming tube. Turn back seams toward inside and close opening with hand stitches.

Step 5. Turn edges of 17" gray square under ¼" and press. Turn under another ¼" and stitch close to turned edges. Fold and place in napkin ring. $

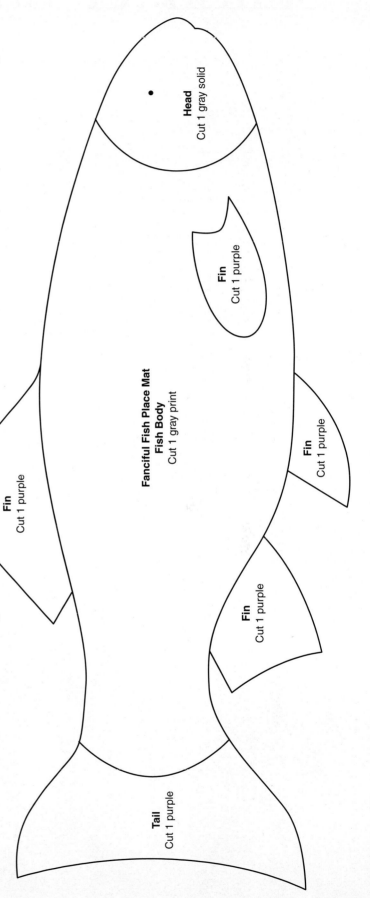

Head
Cut 1 gray solid

Fin
Cut 1 purple

Fanciful Fish Place Mat
Fish Body
Cut 1 gray print

Fin
Cut 1 purple

Fin
Cut 1 purple

Fin
Cut 1 purple

Fin
Cut 1 purple

Tail
Cut 1 purple

Sunflower Buttons Pillow

By Mary Ayres

This project requires little time and investment, but packs a walloping dose of summer and sunshine.

Project Specifications

Skill Level: Beginner

Pillow Size: 14" x 14"

Materials

- 14" pillow form
- 9½" x 9½" square of neutral print or solid for center block
- ½ yard black stripe or print for borders and back
- Assortment of ½"–⅝" brown and black flat buttons
- Assortment of ¼"–½" off-white flat buttons
- Brown and soft yellow 6-strand embroidery floss
- 1¾ yards jumbo black rickrack
- Basic sewing supplies and tools

Instructions

Step 1. From black stripe or print cut two strips each 3" x 9½" and 3" x 14½". Sew shorter strips to two opposite sides of 9½" neutral center square. Sew longer strips to remaining two sides. Press seam allowances toward borders.

Step 2. Transfer sunflower pattern to center square. Using stem stitch, embroider center circle with 3 strands of brown embroidery floss. Embroider petals with 3 strands of soft yellow floss.

Step 3. Arrange buttons on flower center, placing black buttons around edge and brown in the center. Center should be filled and sides of buttons should touch. Sew in place with brown embroidery floss.

Step 4. Arrange off-white buttons on petals, referring to photo for placement. Sew in place with soft yellow floss.

Step 5. Sew black rickrack around pillow front ¼" from edge, beginning and ending in a corner, and stitching through center of rickrack.

Step 6. From black stripe or print cut a square 14½" x 14½". Right sides together, sew pillow front to back along rickrack stitching leaving a 10" opening for turning. Turn right side out, press and insert pillow form. Close opening with hand stitches. $

**Sunflower Buttons Pillow
Sunflower Pattern**

Quick-to-Stitch Surprises

We've all had our share of unexpected gift-giving occasions that we never seem to be prepared for. These cheery gifts fit the bill for just about any occasion, and are fast and fun, too!

Bring a lap robe or a wheelchair tote bag to a nursing home as a gift for an elderly shut-in. Stitch a pretty floral bath set to give to a special friend who's leaving on a cruise—she'll think of you every time she uses it! Or how about stitching a set of sachets as a housewarming gift for your new neighbors?

Any of these gifts are appropriate for any occasion, and each of them can make a special occasion out of an ordinary day. Stitch one for someone you love, just because. Then get ready for hugs!

Beaded Lavender Sachets

By Cindy Gorder

*This trio of fragrant sachets has a decidedly Roaring Twenties look—
sheer, shimmery and with beads galore.*

Project Specifications

Skill Level: Beginner

Hanging Sachet Size: Approximately 4" x 12½"

Round Sachet Size: Approximately 4½" in diameter

Square Sachet Size: Approximately 6" x 6"

Note: Bead counts are approximate. Many of the embellishments are garage sale finds. Feel free to substitute colors and materials that you may find.

Materials

For all Sachets

- 2–3 cups potpourri or lavender buds to fill all three sachets
- Embroidery needle
- Beading thread and needle
- Basic sewing supplies and tools

Hanging Sachet

- Burnout velvet 9" x 11"
- 9" (1¼"-wide) looped fringe trim
- 1 yard each of 2 colors satin ribbon ⅛"-wide
- Long, dangly earring for trim
- 200 purple seed beads
- 21 long purple bugle beads
- 35 short purple bugle beads
- 21 purple rocaille beads

Round Sachet

- Green organza 5" x 5"

- 2 green 5" backing circles
- 2 (1½"-wide) 5" lengths of sheer ribbon in two shades of green
- Typing or tissue paper square 5" x 5"
- 1 yard each light and dark green metallic fine braid embroidery thread
- Small ring-shaped brooch
- 1 (⅝") berry bead
- 105 light green seed beads
- 55 dark green seed beads
- 60 short silver bugle beads
- 60 long green bugle beads
- 30 (³⁄₁₆") small round pearls
- 30 rice pearls
- 1 small green teardrop bead

Square Sachet

- Sheer fabric with leaf motif 6" x 6"
- 26" (1½"-wide) wire-edged variegated ribbon
- Backing fabric 7" x 7"
- 4 (5mm) round copper beads
- 4 (1") long, clear tube beads
- 4 (⅜") green leaf beads
- 8 gold rocaille beads
- 44 (7mm) gold diamond-shaped beads
- 44 small green teardrop beads
- 520 gold seed beads

Instructions

Hanging Sachet

Step 1. Stitch looped fringe trim to one short edge of burnout velvet.

Step 2. With right sides together, using ½" seam allowance, stitch long edges of fabric together. Position seam at center back of tube and stitch across untrimmed end. Turn right side out.

Step 3. Using beading thread and needle, anchor a beading thread at the center of the stitched lower edge of bag. Pick up 5 purple seed beads, a short purple bugle bead, 5 more seed beads, a long purple bugle bead, 5 more seeds, a short purple bugle, 4 more seeds, a rocaille and a final seed. Take the needle back through all but the last seed bead and make one stitch into the fabric. Slide needle left or right ⅛" and repeat the sequence, cutting back to 4 seeds in the first, second and third segments.

Step 4. Continue working away from center, making strands ⅛" apart, and slightly decreasing the number of seed beads each time. When you can no longer decrease seed beads, leave off the last short bugle bead. There should be 10 strands each side of center strand and the three outermost strands, each side, should consist of one seed, short bugle, one seed, long bugle, one seed, rocaille and one seed.

Step 5. Fill pouch to within 2" of top with potpourri or lavender. Knot ⅛"-wide ribbons together with a 4" loop in the center. Tie the ends around the neck of the pouch, pulling tight and knotting to secure. Tie the dangly earring onto one of the ribbon strands.

Round Sachet

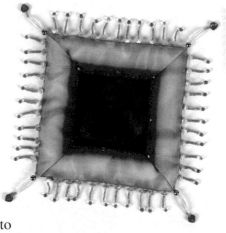

Step 1. Draw a 4" circle on 5" paper square. Place green organza over the circle. Position the two sheer green ribbons at right angles across the center of the circle. Pin all layers to paper. Carefully baste ribbons and organza to paper along drawn circle.

Step 2. Turn piece over and cut away the center of the paper only, being careful not to cut the fabric. Work feather stitch with dark green metallic embroidery braid to attach the edges of one ribbon to the organza. Do not stitch through paper. Use light green metallic fine-braid embroidery thread and buttonhole stitch to attach the other ribbon.

Step 3. With beading thread and needle, sew a light green seed bead at the end of each light green stitch and a dark green seed bead at the end of each dark green stitch.

Step 4. Remove paper very carefully, tearing it away from basting stitches. Dampen slightly if necessary to aid in removal.

Step 5. Cut 1½" off one side of each backing circle. Turn under straight edge of one piece and stitch a narrow hem. Overlap backing pieces to form a 5" circle, and with right sides together, sew front to back. Clip curves and turn right side out.

Step 6. Anchor beading thread anywhere in the perimeter seam. Pick up 2 silver bugle beads and a round pearl. Slide to end of thread next to fabric and take a stitch at the end of the pearl, bringing needle back out next to the bugle bead just behind the pearl. Take needle and thread back through the bugle and pearl, then add two more bugles and one pearl and repeat all the way around the sachet.

Step 7. Bring needle out of a pearl, add one long green bugle, a rice pearl, a dark green seed and two light green seeds; take back through 2 seeds and rice pearl, add another long green bugle, and take thread and needle through next round pearl on sachet. Repeat sequence all around the sachet to make a beaded fringe.

Step 8. Open the back of the sachet and carefully work inside to anchor a doubled beading thread in the center of the top. Bring needle to outside on top and pick up the berry bead and the teardrop. Go back through the berry bead and stitch through both beads once or twice more to anchor them firmly to the fabric.

Step 9. Fill sachet with potpourri or lavender and close the back with hand stitches.

Step 10. Pin the round gold brooch to the top, encircling the berry bead.

Square Sachet

Step 1. Carefully fold and press the wire-edged ribbon at 6" intervals, leaving an extra inch at each end.

Step 2. Form a ribbon border on top of and around the sheer fabric square by folding the ribbon open at a 45-degree angle to miter each corner. Pin in place along the inner edge. Carefully trim ¼"–½" away from the edges of the sheer fabric layer.

Step 3. Press edges of backing fabric ½" to wrong side all around and pin to ribbon and sheer fabric square, wrong sides together.

Step 4. With beading thread and needle, stitch gold seed beads ⅛" apart around three sides of the inner border of the sachet, placing a gold rocaille at each

Continued on page 81

Soft Floral Gift Box

By Patsy Moreland

This pretty fabric box makes a lovely gift by itself, but is also a very feminine presentation for hosiery, cosmetics, lingerie or jewelry.

Project Specifications

Skill Level: Beginner

Box Size: Approximately 9½" x 3¾" x 3½"

Materials

- 2 coordinating floral cotton fabric pieces 16" x 18"
- Cotton batting 16" x 18"
- 2 plastic canvas pieces 3½" x 3¾"
- 4 plastic canvas pieces 3¾" x 9½"
- All-purpose thread to match fabrics
- Water-soluble marker
- #7 embroidery needle
- Low-temperature glue gun and glue sticks
- Embroidered doily, handkerchief or napkin scrap 5" x 6"
- Silk flowers, leaves, ribbon, silk ribbon roses, rhinestones, etc. for embellishment
- Basic sewing supplies and tools

Instructions

Step 1. Bring 18" edges of each fabric piece together, right sides facing; press and pin.

Step 2. Measure and draw outline of half-box on wrong side of folded fabric as shown in Fig. 1. Reset pins through all layers and cut on lines. Unfold fabrics and press.

Step 3. Pin one cut fabric piece on batting and cut a matching shape.

Step 4. Pin right sides of fabric together, batting piece on one wrong side.

Step 5. Start stitching along top edge, 2" from top right corner. Stitch all the way around perimeter as shown in Fig. 2, stopping 2" from top left corner. Carefully clip inner corners.

Step 6. Turn right side out through opening; press.

Step 7. Place plastic canvas between batting and fabric at front through 6" opening. Trim plastic canvas to fit.

Step 8. Gently push plastic canvas to inside seam. Pin and topstitch along plastic canvas edge. Repeat for each section of box.

Step 9. Tuck one edge of embroidered piece into 6" opening. Turn ¼" seam allowances to inside; pin. Close opening with hand stitches.

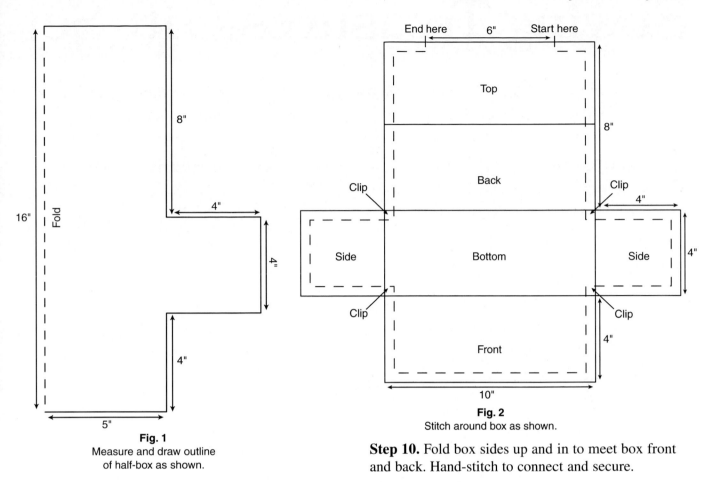

Fig. 1
Measure and draw outline
of half-box as shown.

Fig. 2
Stitch around box as shown.

Step 10. Fold box sides up and in to meet box front and back. Hand-stitch to connect and secure.

Step 11. Hot-glue flowers and embellishments of choice to box. $

Beaded Lavendar Sachets

Continued from page 79

corner and center point. Be sure the stitches go through all fabric layers. Carefully fill the center with potpourri or lavender and bead the last side of the center square.

Step 5. Make an anchoring stitch at one of the outer corners, catching the ribbon and the backing fabric layers. To make a corner bead tassel, add a round copper bead, a clear tube bead, four gold seeds, a leaf bead and another seed. Take the needle back through all but the last seed and make a stitch into the fabric.

Step 6. Slide needle ⅜" away along one edge and make a stitch, catching both fabric layers. Pick up a gold diamond bead, 10 seeds and a green teardrop. Go back through the seeds and gold diamond and make a stitch in the fabric. Slide needle ⅜" away and repeat process. At corners, make the same bead tassel as on the first corner. $

Sewing Treasures Gift Set

By Cindy Gorder

*If you plan to give this set of chatelaine, needle book and scissors fob as a gift,
you will certainly have to plan a second set for yourself. Pretty and practical!*

Project Specifications

Skill Level: Beginner

Chatelaine Size: Approximately 45" x 5"

Needle Book Size: 5" x 4¼"

Scissors Fob Size: 2¼" x 4½"

Note: If your felt has any wool content, you can give it a great fleece-like texture by wetting each piece separately, squeezing out excess water and drying on regular setting of dryer for 35 minutes. Smooth out on a flat surface and allow to dry completely. Some shrinkage will occur, so allow extra felt for large pattern pieces.

Materials

- ⅓ yard purple felt for chatelaine
- 2 pieces of felt 5" x 8½" for needle book cover
- 2 pieces of felt 4½" x 7½" for needle book pages
- Variety of felt scraps for appliqué and embellishment
- 1 yard braided cord for scissors fob
- Buttons in assorted sizes, shapes and colors
- 1 skein purple #3 pearl cotton embroidery thread
- Variety of #8 pearl cotton embroidery threads for embellishment
- Embroidery needle
- Basic sewing supplies and tools

Instructions

Chatelaine

Step 1. Enlarge pattern 222 percent. Trace and cut chatelaine pieces as directed on pattern.

Step 2. From variety of felt scraps cut three pockets for each side of chatelaine in sizes and colors of your choice. Use pattern as a guide for shaping pockets and allow at least 1½" overlap between pockets. Remember to reverse chatelaine pieces to make a left and right side and make pockets to fit each side.

Step 3. Cut assorted appliqué shapes from felt scraps to go on pockets. Treat some shapes as mini-pockets by making them large enough to hold small sewing notions. Appliqué shapes may be circles, triangles,

trapezoids, quarter-moons, tadpoles or any shape you desire.

Step 4. Turn the top edge of each large pocket toward the right side ½"–1" and use buttonhole stitch or feather stitch and #8 pearl cotton in color of your choice to hem in place.

Step 5. Use buttonhole stitch and #8 pearl cotton in color of your choice to sew mini-pockets to each large pocket. Leave the top open, but buttonhole-stitch the top edge to finish.

Step 6. Add buttons to pockets, tying some with thread tails on top for interest.

Step 7. Arrange pockets in overlapping manner on each side of chatelaine, starting at the top and working downward. Stitch upper two pockets in place by sewing across bottom of pocket by hand or machine ¼" from edge. Stack the second pocket so that it overlaps the first to hide the bottom edge. Stitch in place, again overlapping the pocket above.

Step 8. Fill the remaining space above chatelaine halves with appliqués, buttons and embellishments of your choice. Use buttonhole or feather stitch as desired.

Step 9. Connect halves of chatelaine at center back, overlapping ends ½" and using a feather stitch to attach them.

Step 10. Work buttonhole stitch around entire chatelaine with #3 purple pearl cotton. This stitching will attach the bottom pockets to the piece.

Scissors Fob

Step 1. Trace and cut front and back scissors fob pieces from felt scraps of your color choice, adjusting size if necessary to accommodate your own scissors.

Step 2. Cut two appliqué shapes in felt colors of your choice. With feather and/or buttonhole stitch and #8 pearl cotton of your choice attach appliqués to fob front. Add a button. Buttonhole-stitch across top of fob front. Use a different color of pearl cotton to buttonhole-stitch top curved edge of fob back.

Step 3. Using same color of pearl cotton used to stitch

across fob front, buttonhole-stitch front and back together.

Step 4. Stitch ends of braided cord to back of fob where front connects to back. Add a small button to front at each side to cover stitching.

Needle Book

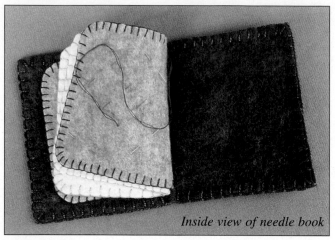

Inside view of needle book

Step 1. Carefully round the corners of the three needle book felt pieces.

Step 2. Fold the 8½" x 5" cover piece in half, bringing short ends together. Mark the center spine with pins or a basting stitch.

Step 3. Cut a few felt appliqué pieces and stitch them to the front cover of the book using buttonhole, feather, chain and straight stitches, overlapping them in a pleasing arrangement. Add some buttons to embellish the front.

Step 4. Place second 8½" x 5" felt piece on wrong side of needle book cover. Work buttonhole stitch with #3 purple pearl cotton around perimeter to hold pieces together.

Step 5. Work buttonhole stitch around two smaller rectangle needle book pages with contrasting #8 pearl cotton.

Step 6. With cover and pages open, center pages on inside of cover and pin. Turn book to outside of cover, and with #3 purple pearl cotton work fly stitch, as shown in Fig. 1, at spine to connect all layers. $

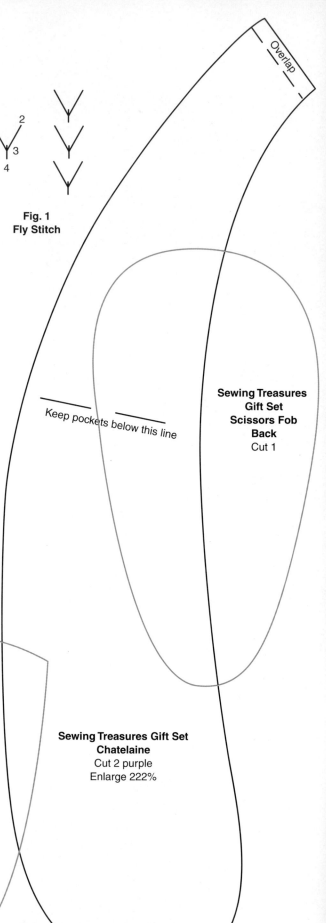

1 2
3
4

**Fig. 1
Fly Stitch**

Overlap

Keep pockets below this line

**Sewing Treasures
Gift Set
Scissors Fob
Back**
Cut 1

**Sewing Treasures Gift Set
Chatelaine**
Cut 2 purple
Enlarge 222%

**Sewing Treasures Gift Set
Scissors Fob
Front**
Cut 1

Tulip Time Bath Set

By Holly Daniels

Pamper yourself or a friend with a gift of this pretty and useful bath set. Present the gift in a woven basket with fragrant soaps or bath gel in coordinating colors.

Project Specifications

Skill Level: Beginner

Back Scrubber Size: 6" x 36"

Soap Holder Size: Approximately 3½" x 4½"

Mitt Size: 7¼" x 9½"

Materials

- Full-size white bath towel
- Scraps of pink and blue print fabrics
- 4 yards purchased or self-made bias binding
- All-purpose threads to match fabrics and towel
- Pink, blue and green 6-strand embroidery floss
- 2 yards 1"-wide sheer green ribbon
- 1½" piece of hook-and-loop tape
- Basic sewing supplies and tools

Instructions

Back Scrubber

Step 1. Cut one piece 6" x 30" from towel.

Step 2. Cut appliqué pieces as instructed on pattern. Referring to photo for placement, center on back scrubber and machine-appliqué with satin stitch and matching thread to secure all raw edges.

Step 3. With 3 strands of green embroidery floss, stem-stitch lines radiating from flowers. Make French knots where indicated by dots on pattern, using 3 strands of pink or blue embroidery floss. Wrap floss around needle three times for French knots.

Step 4. Cut three 12" lengths of sheer green ribbon. Tie three bows and tack to bottom of each flower.

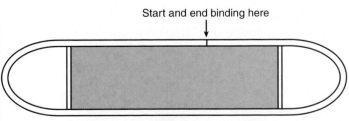

Fig. 1
Attach binding to back scrubber as
shown, leaving 12" loop at each end.

Start and end binding here

Step 5. Cut two 6" lengths of bias binding. Bind short edges of scrubber. Cut a piece of bias binding 85" long. Begin binding a few inches from the end of one long side of scrubber. Leave 12" of binding unattached at each end as shown in Fig. 1. Fold the 12" unattached binding piece edges together and close with hand stitches.

Soap Holder

Step 1. Cut piece of towel 5½" x 10". Use curve pattern to round one end (top) of strip. Finish other end with overcast or zigzag stitch.

Step 2. Sew loop side of hook-and-loop tape on outside of holder as shown in Fig. 2.

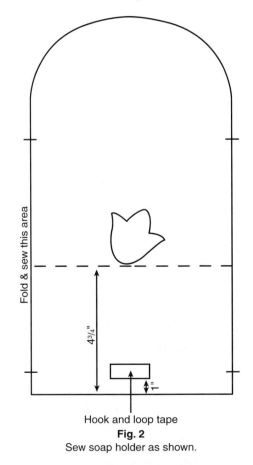

Fold & sew this area

4¾"

1"

Hook and loop tape
Fig. 2
Sew soap holder as shown.

Step 3. Trace and cut appliqué as instructed on pattern. Appliqué and embroider as in Steps 2 and 3 of Back Scrubber.

Step 4. Fold piece, right sides together, and sew sides together using ½" seam allowance, again referring to Fig. 2.

Step 5. Bind curved edge with 8" piece of bias binding.

Step 6. Insert soap into holder. Fold flap to check placement and sew other strip of hook-and-loop tape to inside of flap.

Step 7. Cut 12" length of sheer green ribbon. Tie in bow and tack to lower edge of flower.

Mitt

Step 1. Cut two mitt pieces from towel. Trace and cut flower as indicated on pattern. Appliqué and embroider as in Steps 2 and 3 of Back Scrubber.

Step 2. Place mitt pieces wrong sides together and pin. Bind mitt edges together with bias binding. Bind hand opening to finish.

Step 3. Cut 12" length of sheer green ribbon. Tie in bow and tack to lower edge of flower. $

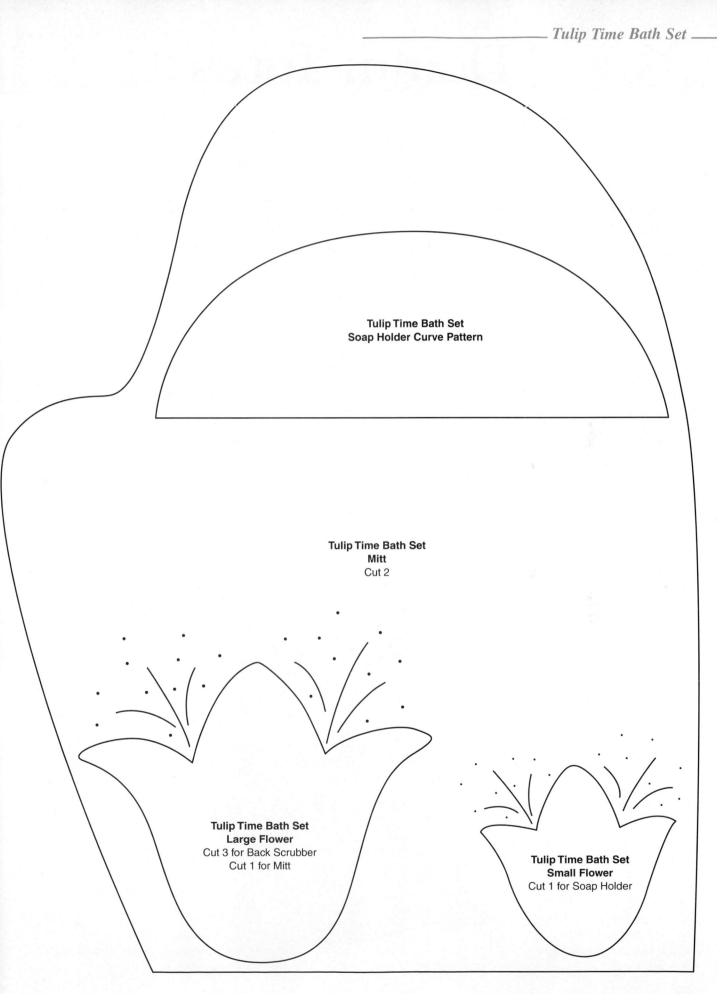

Tulip Time Bath Set
Soap Holder Curve Pattern

Tulip Time Bath Set
Mitt
Cut 2

Tulip Time Bath Set
Large Flower
Cut 3 for Back Scrubber
Cut 1 for Mitt

Tulip Time Bath Set
Small Flower
Cut 1 for Soap Holder

Denim Totes

By Patsy Moreland

Two roomy bags made from recycled denim jeans. The only purchases necessary will be buckles and webbing needed to attach strap and fasten to wheelchair.

Project Specifications

Skill Level: Beginner

Shoulder Bag Size: Approximately 8¾" x 11¾"

Wheelchair Tote Size: 11¾" x 22" (varies with size of jeans)

Materials

- 1 pair recycled denim jeans for each tote
- All-purpose thread to match denim
- 1 pair side-snap buckles 1¼" x 2¾" for wheelchair tote; single buckle for shoulder bag
- ¾ yard 1"-wide webbing
- Water-soluble marker
- #7 embroidery needle
- Basic sewing supplies and tools

Instructions

Shoulder Bag

Note: This shoulder bag uses only one leg of one pair of jeans and does not include zipper area.

Step 1. On one side of zipper area measure from the top of the waistband down one leg 12" and mark with water-soluble marker. Repeat from top of waistband at side seam. Connect marks with a straight line. Cut off bottom leg fabric one thickness at a time.

Step 2. Measure from side seam, below waistband, horizontally toward zipper area and mark at 9". Measure and mark at bottom of side seam 11". Pin pocket lining up out of the way. Connect marks and cut off one layer at a time.

Step 3. Pin, right sides together, and sew with ¼" seam allowance down front, pivot and sew across bottom. Stitch twice and turn right side out.

Step 4. Cut a strip at leg side seam ¾" x 45", piecing if necessary.

Step 5. Cut and sew a 3" piece of leg seam strip to inside of waistband close to side seam. Thread end of strip through the single-opening hole of buckle and bring end of strip to outside of waistband. Stitch three times to firmly secure.

Step 6. Sew one end of remainder of leg side seam strip to inside of waistband at the other side of opening. Thread the other end of the strip through the lower opening of the adjustable end of the buckle, over the bar and out the top opening as shown in Fig. 1. Turn under ½" at the end of the strip and stitch. This end is the lock to keep the strap from pulling out. Strap is adjusted from this end of the buckle.

Wheelchair Tote

Note: This tote uses the entire top of jeans and includes zipper area.

Step 1. Turn jeans inside out. Measure 12" down from top of waistband at each side seam and center front. Mark with water-soluble marker. Connect marks with line.

Step 2. Cut one fabric thickness on marked line, then use as guide for cutting back fabric.

Step 3. Pin right sides together at cut edges. Stitch with ¼" seam allowance. Repeat stitching on same line.

Step 4. Using #7 embroidery needle and doubled sewing thread, sew zipper placket closed on right side of jeans.

Step 5. Cut two 5" pieces of webbing. Turn one end under 1½". Thread through one-hole opening of buckle and stitch through both thicknesses of webbing several times to secure. Repeat for second buckle.

Step 6. Turn other end under 1" and stitch to wrong side of front waistband 2" from side seam. Repeat with other buckle 2" from other side seam.

Step 7. Cut two 7" pieces of webbing. Thread over and under the bar at other end of buckle. Pull enough through to turn under ½" and machine-stitch securely. Turn under the other end 1" and stitch to wrong side of back waistband 2" from side seam. Repeat with second strip, sewing 2" from other side of back waistband.

Step 8. Thread other end of strip from under the buckle, through the hole and over the bar. Pull enough of the end through to turn under ½". Stitch securely. Strap is adjusted from this end of buckle. $

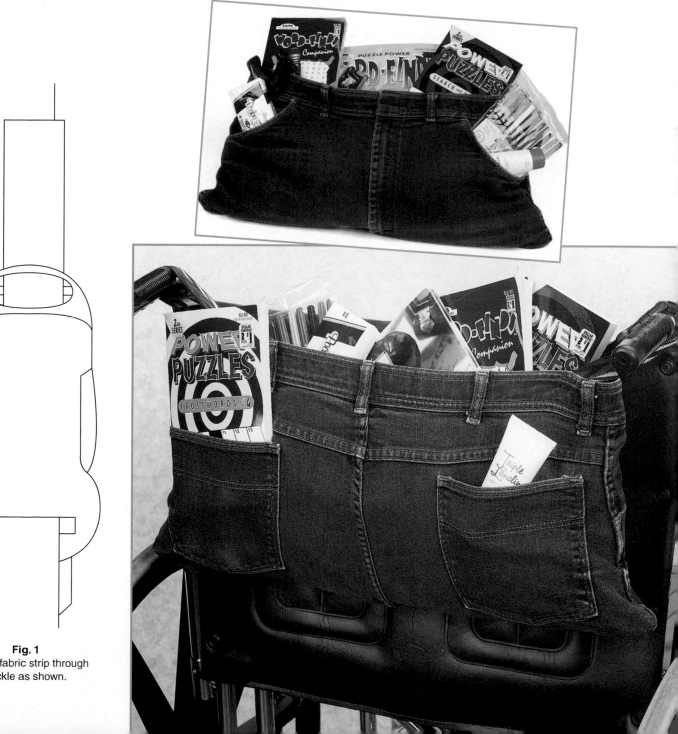

Fig. 1
Thread fabric strip through buckle as shown.

Pretty Posies Pillow

By Thaea Lloyd

This piece has a primitive quality. Don't be afraid to improvise with irregular shapes and change of proportions. If you want to change a color, add a flower, bend a stem … do it! Make it your own work of art.

Project Specifications

Skill Level: Beginner

Pillow Size: 18" x 18"

Note: The appliqué pieces for this pillow were cut entirely from pieces of recycled wool. Beg and borrow scraps from all your friends who sew, and search thrift shops for color and texture. If you don't have wool, substitute felt.

Materials

- 18" x 18" pillow covered with dark fabric
- 12" x 12" wool for background of appliqué design
- Assorted colors of wool for design elements
- Assorted colors of 6-strand embroidery floss
- All-purpose green and blue sewing thread
- Glue stick
- Basic sewing supplies and tools

Instructions

Step 1. Cut design elements from wool or felt. Because wool and felt keep a clean edge when cut, turn-under allowances do not have to be added. Overlap allowances do need to be considered for some pieces, however.

Step 2. Referring to pattern and photo, arrange pieces on 12" x 12" background for appliqué design. Pin or lightly glue in place.

Step 3. With blue and green threads, machine-stitch parallel rows of stitches on stems and veins on leaves.

Step 4. Sew flower pieces in place with buttonhole stitch and two strands of matching or contrasting embroidery floss.

Step 5. Attach flower centers with 3–5 French knots in contrasting colors.

Step 6. Trim away the appliqué background square leaving ⅛"–¼" around pieces.

Step 7. Hand-appliqué completed piece to pillow top. $

Pretty Posies Pillow
Appliqué Pattern
Enlarge 118%

Victorian Sachet Slippers

By Karen Mead

These trimmed lady's slippers are both whimsical and unique. They would make a lovely bridal shower gift or a send-off for a traveling friend.

Project Specifications

Skill Level: Beginner

Slipper Size: Approximately 8½" x 3"

Materials

Note: Materials are for all three slippers.

- Scraps of gray, green, black and burgundy fabrics
- Buttons, scraps of ribbon, lace, assorted trims and embellishments
- Scraps of fusible transfer web
- 1 yard (⅛"-wide) burgundy satin ribbon
- All-purpose threads to match fabrics
- ¾ cup potpourri or dried lavender
- Polyester fiberfill
- Fabric glue
- Basic sewing supplies and tools

Instructions

Black Shoe

Step 1. Fold gray fabric scrap in half, wrong sides together. Trace and cut pattern for black shoe.

Step 2. Trace heel and toe pattern on paper side of fusible transfer web. Cut out leaving roughly ½" margin around traced lines. Following manufacturer's instructions, fuse to black fabric and cut out on traced lines. Fuse to gray shoe as indicated on pattern.

Step 3. Stitch a strip of lace trim onto ankle opening on shoe front with ⅛" seam.

Step 4. Cut an 8" piece of ⅛"-wide ribbon for hanger.

Step 5. Pin right sides of shoe together. Tuck lace into shoe and pin ribbon hanger in place on the heel of the shoe. Stitch around perimeter using ¼" seam allowance. Leave bottom of heel open. Turn right side out.

Step 6. Stuff toe area of shoe lightly with polyester fiberfill. Pour in about two tablespoons of potpourri. Continue stuffing with fiberfill. Close heel opening with hand stitches.

Step 7. Stitch ⅛"-wide burgundy satin ribbon along bottom of lace and tie a small bow from same ribbon to accent vamp.

Green Shoe

Step 1. Fold green fabric scrap in half, wrong sides together. Trace and cut pattern for green shoe.

Step 2. Trace heel and toe pattern on paper side of fusible web. Cut out leaving roughly ½" margin around traced lines. Following manufacturer's instructions, fuse to darker green fabric and

Toe Trim
Cut 1 black

Victorian Sachet Slippers
Black Shoe
Cut 2 gray—entire shoe

Heel Trim
Cut 1 black

Leave open to stuff

cut out on traced lines. Fuse to green shoe as indicated on pattern.

Step 3. Stitch and stuff as in Black Shoe, Steps 5 and 6.

Step 4. Stitch four buttons on top of shoe.

Burgundy Shoe

Step 1. Fold burgundy fabric scrap in half, wrong sides together. Trace and cut pattern for burgundy shoe.

Step 2. Trace insert on paper side of fusible transfer web. Cut out leaving roughly ½" margin around traced lines. Following manufacturer's instructions, fuse to gray fabric and cut out on traced lines. Fuse to burgundy shoe as indicated on pattern.

Step 3. Stitch ⅛"-wide burgundy ribbon along front of shoe as shown on pattern.

Step 4. Stitch and stuff as in Black Shoe, Steps 5 and 6.

Step 5. Stitch small lace doily or similar trim on toe of shoe. Glue button at center of trim. $

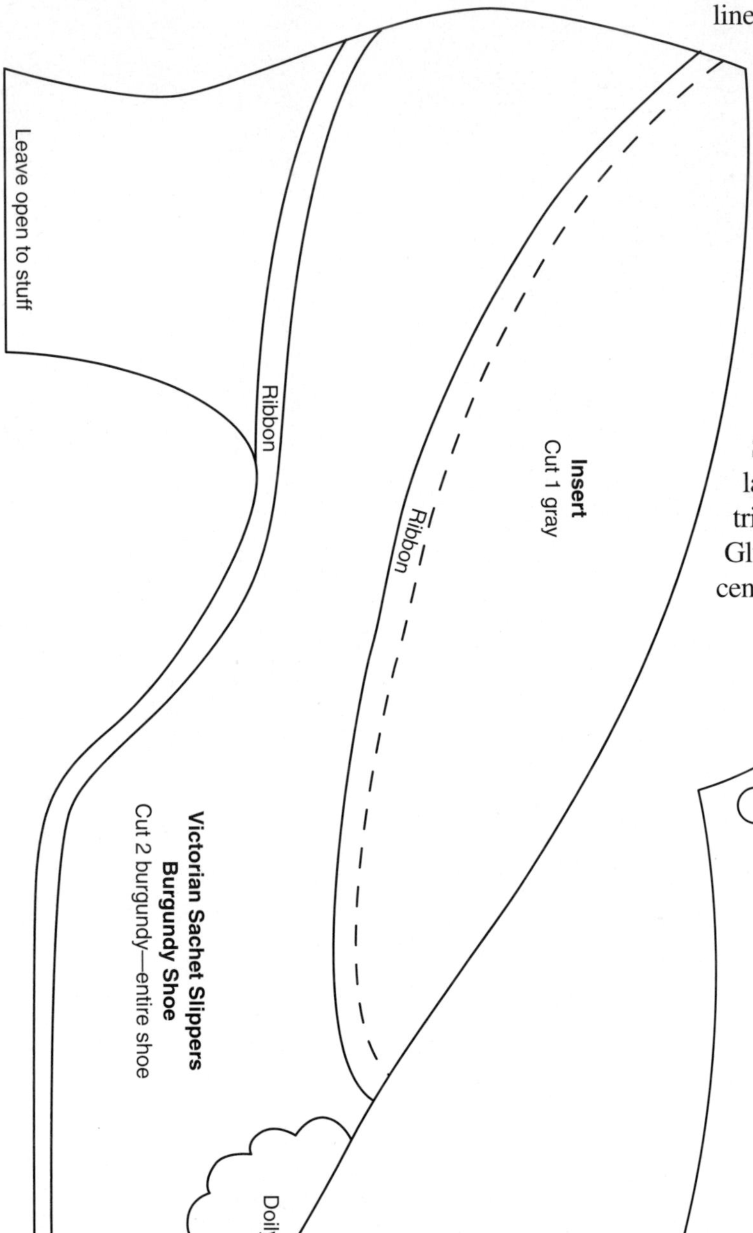

Leave open to stuff

Ribbon

Ribbon

Insert
Cut 1 gray

**Victorian Sachet Slippers
Burgundy Shoe**
Cut 2 burgundy—entire shoe

Doily

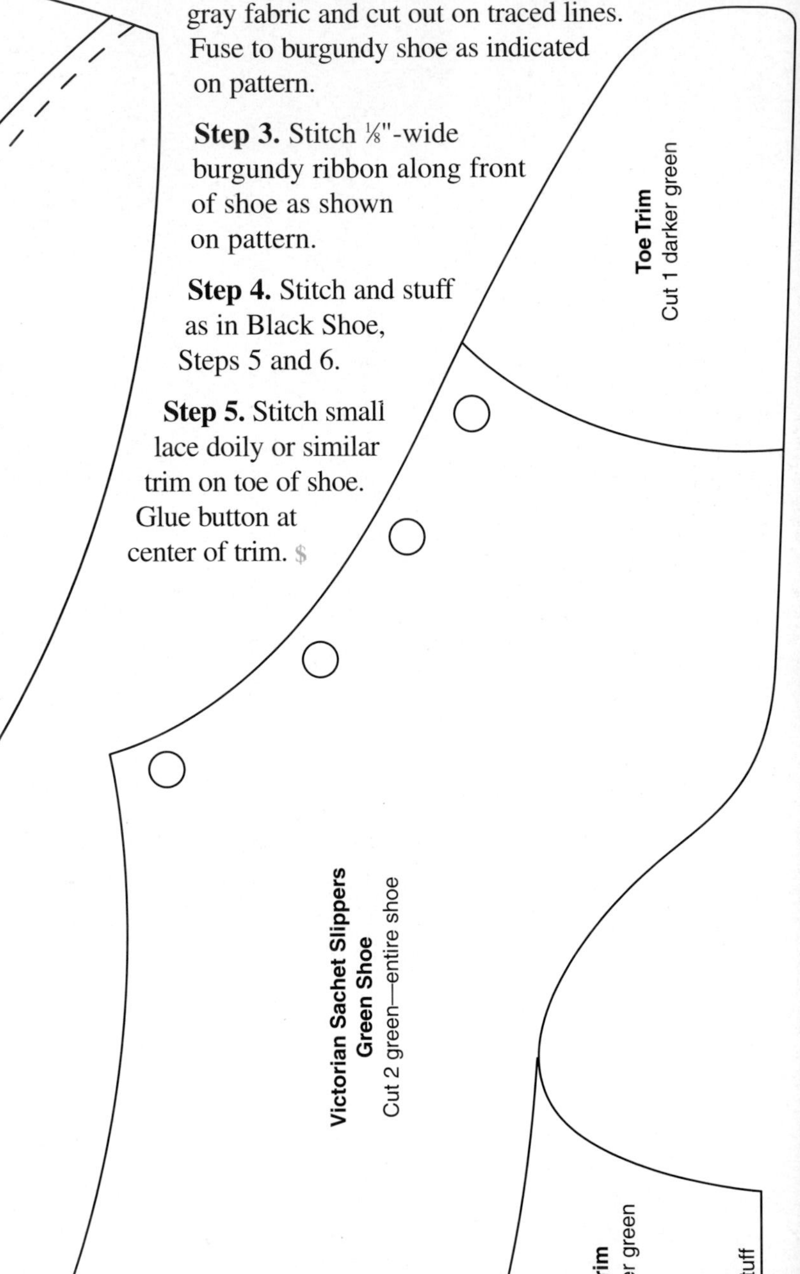

Toe Trim
Cut 1 darker green

**Victorian Sachet Slippers
Green Shoe**
Cut 2 green—entire shoe

Heel Trim
Cut 1 darker green

Leave open to stuff

Pocket Pal Coin Purses

By Cathy Hallier

Just the right size to carry a credit card, key and money when a bulky purse might be a burden. For a gift, add some money, a photo or meaningful trinkets.

Project Specifications

Skill Level: Beginner

Coin Purse Size: Approximately 4" x 3"

Materials

- 2 pieces of fabric 4½" x 8½"
- Thin batting piece 4½" x 6½"
- 1 (¾") button
- All-purpose thread to match fabric
- Basic sewing supplies and tools

Instructions

Step 1. Place two fabric pieces on work surface, right sides together, and place batting piece on top. Align three sides, leaving 2" of fabric exposed at top; pin.

Step 2. Fold in corners of 2" exposed fabric (both layers) as shown in Fig. 1: press. Cut away corner pieces of fabric on fold lines and repin.

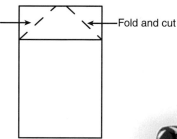

Fold and cut — Fold and cut

Fig. 1
Fold corners of fabric as shown and cut.

Step 3. Machine-stitch around perimeter, leaving opening on one side for turning.

Step 4. Trim corners and turn right side out; press.

Step 5. Fold lower edge up to meet 2" extension at top. Starting at top as shown in Fig. 2, top-stitch one side, enclosing opening in seam, across bottom and up other side.

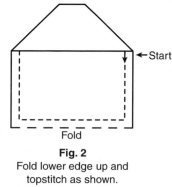

← Start

Fold

Fig. 2
Fold lower edge up and topstitch as shown.

Step 6. Center and work buttonhole in fabric flap. Sew button on front of purse, aligning with buttonhole. $

Embellished Closet Safe

By Karen Mead

Created from a pretty vintage linen pillowcase, this item is a bit unusual and makes a very special gift. It helps alleviate closet clutter by providing storage for accessories.

Project Specifications

Skill Level: Beginner

Closet Safe Size: Approximately 13½" x 17½

Materials

- White plastic garment hanger
- Vintage embellished pillowcase
- 16" white zipper
- ⅓ yard ¼"-wide ribbon to match pillowcase
- Basic sewing supplies and tools

Instructions

Step 1. Open all three seams of pillowcase.

Step 2. With the pillowcase front folded in half lengthwise, measure from the embellished edge up 15" and cut as shown in Fig. 1.

Step 3. Measure 1½" above design area and cut again as shown in Fig. 2.

Step 4. Right sides together, stitch this cut back together with ½" seam allowance and basting-length machine stitch. Center and stitch 16" zipper into this seam following directions on zipper package.

Step 5. With pillowcase back folded in half lengthwise, measure from embellished edge up 14" and cut.

Step 6. Right sides together, fold front and back together lengthwise and measure down 4". Place a pin as a marker. Using a ruler, draw a line from top of center fold to pin as shown in Fig. 3. Cut through all layers on this marked line.

Step 7. With right sides together, layers open flat, stitch all around perimeter, starting and stopping at center top and leaving a 1" opening for hanger.

Step 8. Turn pillowcase through zipper opening and insert hanger in opening at center top. Hand-stitch ¼"-wide ribbon around opening to finish. Tie bow in front of pillowcase. $

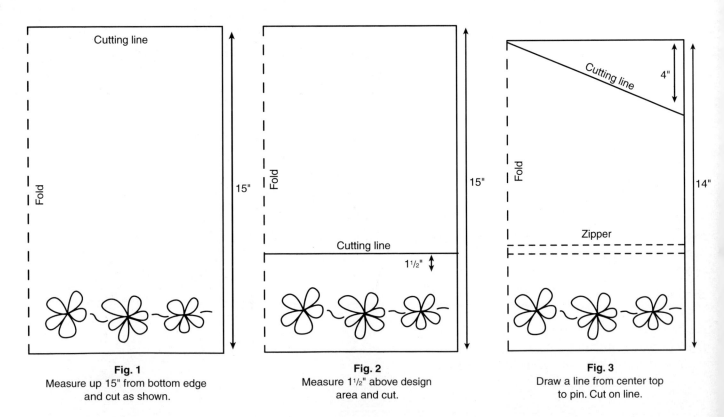

Fig. 1
Measure up 15" from bottom edge and cut as shown.

Fig. 2
Measure 1½" above design area and cut.

Fig. 3
Draw a line from center top to pin. Cut on line.

Welcoming Baby

It always seems to happen that several of your friends or family members are expecting babies at the same time, and each of them deserves a hand-sewn gift made especially for her!

In this chapter you'll find special gifts for all the babies being born in your family or circle of friends. The Chubby Ducky will make both Mom and Baby coo with delight, and the Playful Pals Bibs will protect Baby's clothes during meals. After Baby's done playing, Mom will love putting all the toys in a toy bag made with love by you.

Make one or make several— these projects are inexpensive and fast, but look like you purchased them in an exclusive baby boutique!

Chubby Ducky

By Mary Ayres

No bathtub for this yellow ducky! He's a bright, wonderfully snuggly dry-land friend for baby.

Project Specifications

Skill Level: Beginner

Ducky Size: Approximately 7" x 7"

Materials

- Yellow chenille 20" x 20"
- 2 squares orange felt 2¼" x 2¼"
- 2 (¼") black beads
- ½ yard (1½"-wide) plaid ribbon
- Black 6-strand embroidery floss
- Polyester fiberfill
- Pinking shears
- Basic sewing supplies and tools

Instructions

Step 1. Cut a 12" circle from yellow chenille for duck body. Sew a basting stitch around the circle, close to the edge. Pull stitches tightly to gather and knot to secure. Fill body firmly and evenly with polyester fiberfill.

Step 2. Cut a 6" circle from chenille for duck head. Sew a basting stitch around the circle, close to the edge. Pull stitches tightly to gather and knot to secure. Fill head firmly and evenly with polyester fiberfill. Sew gathered end of head to gathered end of body with invisible stitches.

Step 3. Place two squares of orange felt together and stitch ⅜" from all edges. Trim with pinking shears. Fold squares in half diagonally. To make nostrils, embroider a French knot on each side of beak, close to folded edge. See photo for placement. Make knots through all layers, wrapping 6 strands of black embroidery floss around needle one time for each knot.

Step 4. Sew folded edge of beak to center front of face, using invisible stitches. Using matching sewing thread, sew ¼" black beads to face for eyes, centering them ¼" above beak and hiding knots under beak.

Step 5. Cut two 6½" circles from yellow chenille for wings. Fold circles in half and cut along fold. Sew wings together in pairs along rounded sides ¼" from edge. Turn right side out. Turn raw edges in ¼". Sew a basting stitch along turned-in edges on each wing. Pull stitches tightly to gather. Knot to secure. Sew gathered edges symmetrically to sides of duck, at joining of head and body.

Step 6. Tie ribbon in a bow. Trim ends. Sew bow to center front of duck's neck. $

Playful Pals Bibs

By Mary Ayres

Two adorable designs to sew quickly and inexpensively for someone's sweet new baby.

Project Specifications

Skill Level: Beginner

Bib Size: Approximately 8½" x 8½"

Materials

- Small pieces of pastel plaids and checks for bib fronts, backs and ears
- 2½ yards white or off-white piping
- 2 yards white or off-white double-fold bias tape
- 2 (⅞") pastel two-hole flat buttons
- 4 (½") black two-hole flat buttons
- 2 pieces of thin cotton batting 9" x 9"
- Black 6-strand embroidery floss
- White all-purpose sewing thread
- Basic sewing supplies and tools

Instructions

Dog Bib

Step 1. Using dog pattern trace and cut bib and ear pieces as directed on pattern.

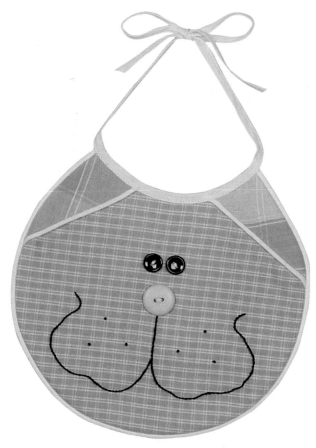

Step 2. Transfer face details to one bib piece. With 3 strands of black embroidery floss, work outline stitch on muzzle lines and French knots on muzzle dots, wrapping floss around needle three times for each knot.

Step 3. Sew ⅞" button for nose to center top of muzzle with white thread. Holes should be placed horizontally. Place eye buttons as indicated on pattern, angling top button holes inward. Sew with white all-purpose sewing thread.

Step 4. Sew piping around side and bottom of face, ¼" from edge.

Step 5. Place batting on work surface. Place dog face and lining right sides together on top of batting. Sew along piping stitching, leaving neck edge open. Turn right side out.

Step 6. Sew piping around sides and bottom edge of one ear and one ear reversed ¼" from edge. Right sides together, sew ear fronts to ear backs along piping stitching. Leave tops open. Turn right side out and baste to top of face as shown on pattern.

Step 7. Cut a 32" length from double-fold bias tape. Find center and match to center front of bib. Sew to lining side of neck edge. Fold tape over to front of bib. Sew ties and neck edge close to fold edges.

Cat Bib

Step 1. Using cat pattern, trace, cut and sew as in Steps 1–3 of Dog Bib.

Step 2. Sew piping along lower edges of ears ¼" from edge. Position ears at top of bib and sew to bib along piping stitching. Press seam allowances toward ears. Baste in place along outer edge of bib.

Step 3. Sew piping around side and bottom of face, ¼" from edge.

Step 4. Finish as for Dog Bib, Steps 5–7. $

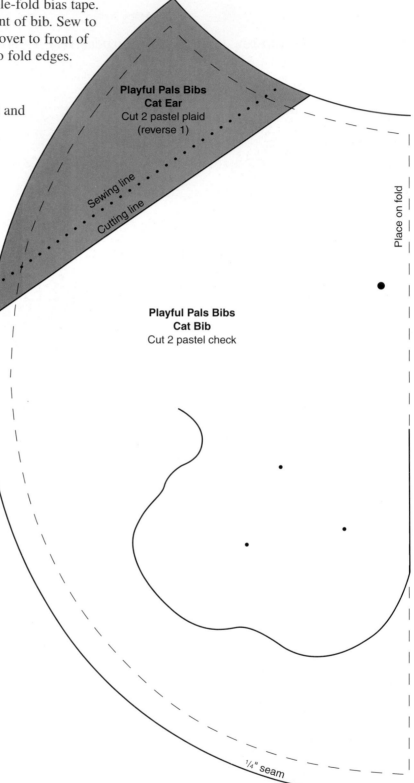

Playful Pals Bibs
Cat Ear
Cut 2 pastel plaid
(reverse 1)

Sewing line

Cutting line

Place on fold

Playful Pals Bibs
Cat Bib
Cut 2 pastel check

¼" seam

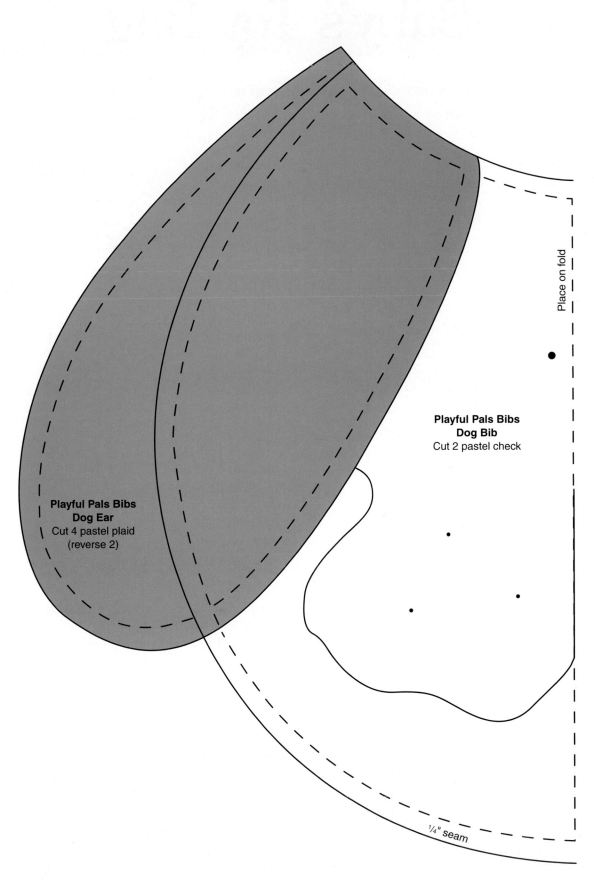

**Playful Pals Bibs
Dog Bib**
Cut 2 pastel check

Place on fold

**Playful Pals Bibs
Dog Ear**
Cut 4 pastel plaid
(reverse 2)

¼" seam

Baby's Toy Bag

By Karen Mead

*New moms will be delighted with this thoughtful gift—
and so will you with the ease with which it is made!*

Project Specifications

Skill Level: Beginner

Toy Bag Size: Approximately 16" x 25"

Materials

- Recycled crib sheet or 1 yard baby-print fabric
- 3" x 3" squares of blue, pink, green and yellow felt
- Scraps of white felt for letters
- White 6-strand embroidery floss
- 1⅓ yards white cotton cord
- Small safety pin
- Basic sewing supplies and tools

Instructions

Step 1. From baby print fabric cut one piece 26" x 33" for bag and one strip 1½" x 33" for cord pocket. Press under each long edge of cord pocket strip ¼".

Step 2. Bring 26" sides of fabric piece together, right sides facing. Stitch bottom and side of bag with ¼" seam.

Step 3. Trace and cut letters from white felt. Place one letter on each colored felt square. Using 2 strands of white embroidery floss, buttonhole-stitch each letter to a colored felt square.

Step 4. Turn top edge of bag under ¼" twice. Press and stitch for hem.

Step 5. Turn bag right side out. Using photo as a guide, pin felt blocks in place. Using 2 strands of white embroidery floss, button-hole-stitch each block to front of bag.

Step 6. Inside bag, measure down 3" and pin cord pocket strip around bag, wrong sides facing. Stitch both top and bottom edge of strip in place as shown in Fig. 1.

Step 7. Turn bag right side out and cut two small slits on each side of toy bag between top and bottom stitch line of cord pocket as shown in Fig. 2.

Step 8. Cut piece of cotton cord in half. Pin a small safety pin to one end of one piece of cord and use to string cord all around bag, coming out at same side where started as shown in Fig. 3. Weave the second cord through cord pocket, starting and ending at the other side of bag. Tie two strands protruding at each side into a simple knot. $

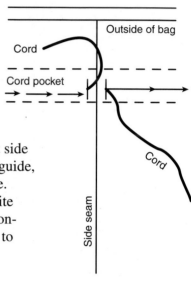

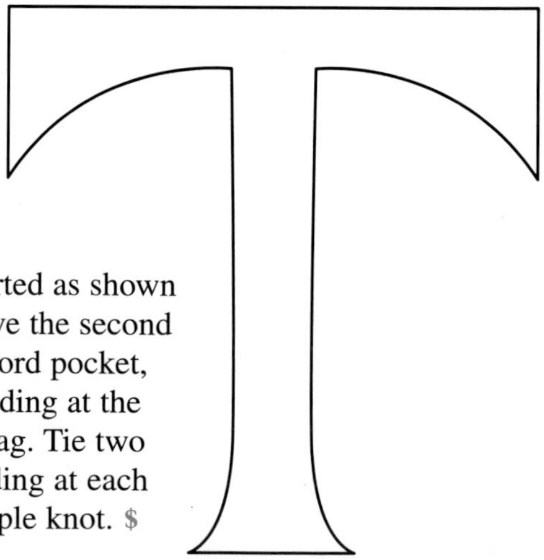

Fig. 3
Thread each cord through pocket as shown.

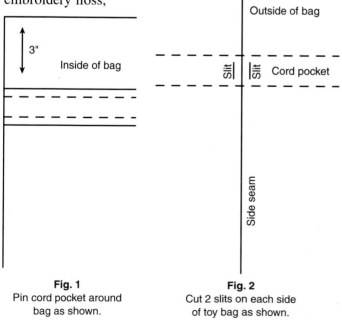

Fig. 1
Pin cord pocket around bag as shown.

Fig. 2
Cut 2 slits on each side of toy bag as shown.

**Baby's Toy Bag
Letter T**
Cut 1 white felt

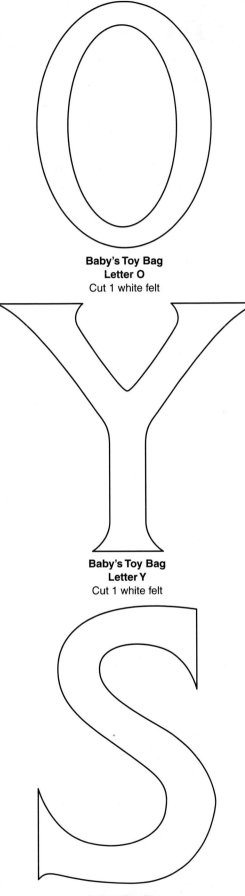

Baby's Toy Bag
Letter O
Cut 1 white felt

Baby's Toy Bag
Letter Y
Cut 1 white felt

Baby's Toy Bag
Letter S
Cut 1 white felt

Baby Blocks Bib

By Julie Weaver

Watch for a sale on hand towels and make a practical, fun, colorful and inexpensive gift for baby.

Project Specifications

Skill Level: Beginner

Bib Size: Approximately 12" x 12½"

Materials

- 1 purchased hand towel at least 12" x 25"
- ¾ yard bright print fabric for bands, binding and ties
- Scraps of fabric in coordinating bright colors
- Scraps of fusible transfer web
- Machine-appliqué threads to match fabric scraps
- Scraps of stabilizer
- Red 6-strand embroidery floss
- Basic sewing supplies and tools

Instructions

Step 1. Trim towel to measure 12" x 25".

Step 2. From print fabric cut a strip 4" x 28". With right sides facing, fold the strip in half lengthwise. Sew the long side with a ¼" seam. Turn right side out and press so seam is at center back. Cut strip in half and sew one strip over the woven band at each end of the towel. Trim even with the sides.

Step 3. Fold towel in half, short ends together. Use pattern to cut a neck opening appropriate for the size of the child. Stay-stitch neck opening. Fold towel in half lengthwise and cut center back opening from neck opening to end of towel as shown in Fig. 1.

Step 4. From the bright print fabric, cut three strips 2½" x 42" to make binding. Join strips end to end. Press in half lengthwise, wrong sides together. Beginning at one side of back opening, right sides facing, sew binding all around towel and back to other side of back opening with ⅜" seam. Turn binding strip to back of towel and slipstitch in place.

Step 5. Measure around neck opening. Add this measurement to 58" and make 2½"-wide bias binding this length. Wrong sides together, press binding strip in half lengthwise. Cut four 7" lengths for side ties. Fold these strips lengthwise in thirds, raw edges to the inside, and sew.

Step 6. Match the center of the remaining bias strip with the center front of neck edge. Right sides facing, pin to neck edge. Starting at center back edge, sew binding around neck opening. Fold binding to wrong side and slipstitch in place.

Step 7. Sew folded edges of binding together each side of center back for ties.

Step 8. Trace appliqué shapes on paper side of fusible transfer web as instructed on patterns. Cut out leaving roughly ½" around each piece. Following manufacturer's instructions, fuse to selected fabrics. Cut out on traced lines.

Step 9. Referring to photo for placement, arrange appliqué pieces on bib front; fuse. Pin stabilizer to wrong side of bib in appliqué areas. Use machine satin-stitch and matching appliqué threads to stitch around each shape.

Step 10. Write numerals 1, 2 and 3 on front of blocks. With two strands of red embroidery floss, embroider numerals using chain stitch as shown in Fig. 2.

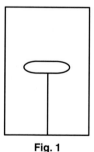

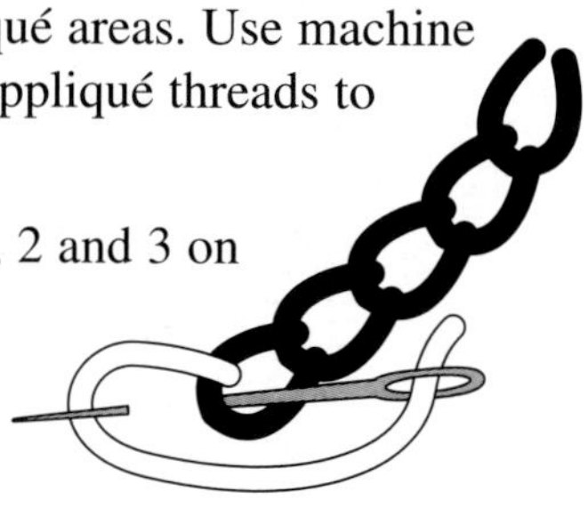

Fig. 2
Chain Stitch

Step 11. Bring short ends of bib together, folding in half. Measure down 4" on each side from shoulder. With thread that matches towel, machine-stitch a 1¼"-long

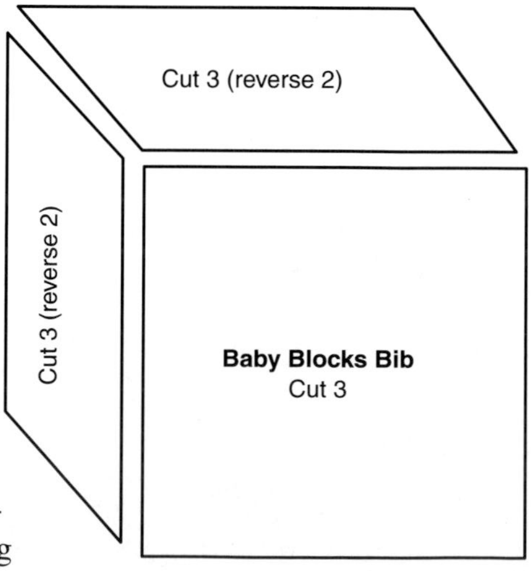

Fig. 1
Cut center back opening as shown.

Cut 3 (reverse 2)

Cut 3 (reverse 2)

Baby Blocks Bib
Cut 3

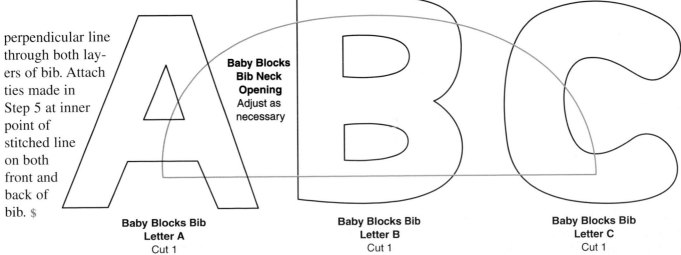

Back view of bib

perpendicular line through both layers of bib. Attach ties made in Step 5 at inner point of stitched line on both front and back of bib. $

Baby Blocks Bib Neck Opening
Adjust as necessary

Baby Blocks Bib Letter A
Cut 1

Baby Blocks Bib Letter B
Cut 1

Baby Blocks Bib Letter C
Cut 1

Pretty as a Picture

By June Fiechter

Ever think about recycling fabrics? Visit your local thrift shop with this goal in mind. Children's clothing can easily be cut from gently worn adult clothing.

Project Specifications

Skill Level: Beginner

Size: Toddler's medium

Materials

- New Look Pattern for Kids #6367
- Recycled fabric in coordinating floral and small plaid
- Buttons and notions as required by pattern
- Thread to match fabrics
- 1 (1⅛") wooden flower craft button
- Acrylic paints to embellish flower button
- Green machine-embroidery thread
- Basic sewing supplies and tools

Instructions

Dress

Step 1. Cut apart recycled garments at seam lines. Press flat. Place commercial pattern pieces on fabric. Use small plaid for dress and sleeve band and floral for sleeves and bib. Cut and construct following pattern directions, but do not add hem.

Step 2. From floral fabric cut a bias strip 1½" x 48". Fold each long edge to the center and press. Bring folded edges together and press again. Aligning raw edges, sew bias strip to wrong side of lower edges of skirt. Fold to front and finish with narrow zigzag stitch.

Bib

Step 1. Cut bib from floral fabric as directed on pattern. From floral fabric cut a strip 1¾" x 45", piecing as necessary. Fold under one long edge ¼"; press. Turn under ¼" again, press and stitch for hem. Sew a long gathering stitch on unfinished long edge. Pull and gather to fit outer edge of bib.

Step 2. Right sides together, pin gathered ruffle to outer edge of bib. Place right side of lining to right side of bib, ruffle between. Stitch around all edges, except neckline. Turn right side out and press. Baste neckline edges of bib together.

Step 3. From small plaid fabric cut a bias strip 1½" x 32". Fold each long edge to the center and press. Bring folded edges together and press again. Find center of folded bias strip and match to center front of bib. Aligning raw edges, sew to lining side of neck edge. Fold tape over to front of bib. Sew ties and neck edge close to fold with a narrow zigzag stitch. Turn ends of ties in to finish.

Step 4. Machine-embroider three small leaves at center front of bib. Paint wooden flower craft button in colors to coordinate with bib. Sew to center front over embroidered leaves. $

**Pretty as a Picture Dress
Bib
Cut 2**

Place on fold

Center Front

Harvest Gatherings

A chill is in the air and the frost is on the pumpkin, and that can only mean one thing—family celebrations in an atmosphere full of love!

Harvest holidays include back-to-school celebrations, Halloween and Thanksgiving; in this chapter are presents galore for all of these gift-giving occasions. Stitch up a tea cozy to be enjoyed while the cold wind is blowing frost on the leaves. A pumpkin-patch car coat will make certain your favorite little one stays warm. A comical turkey wall hanging will bring grins and giggles to the charmed recipient.

And don't you deserve a special gift, too, for all the stitching you've done for others throughout the year? Make the Autumn Breeze Sweatshirt Jacket just for you!

Bushel of Apples Pincushions

By Julie G. DeGroat

Because they are fun to make and useful, too, you will want to keep sewing apples until you indeed have a bushel to give away!

Project Specifications

Skill Level: Beginner

Pincushion Size: Approximately 3" x 3" x 3"

Note: Materials are for one pincushion

Materials

- 14" x 14" square of homespun
- 7" x 7" square of green felt
- 1 (⅞") button
- All-purpose thread to match fabric
- Heavy quilting or button thread
- Long doll needle
- Polyester fiberfill
- Basic sewing supplies and tools

Bushel of Apples Pincushions
Leaf
Cut 4 green felt

Bushel of Apples Pincushions
Apple
Cut 4 homespun

¼" seam allowance

Instructions

Step 1. Cut out fabric pieces as directed on patterns.

Step 2. Sew apple pieces together in pairs, following curve. Sew two pairs together in the same manner, leaving a small opening at the top for stuffing. Clip curves, turn right side out and stuff firmly with polyester fiberfill. Close opening with hand stitches.

Step 3. Place two leaf pieces together and sew ¼" seam around shape with straight or zigzag stitch. Make two.

Step 4. With heavy thread stitch leaves, points overlapping, to apple top at sewn closure. Knot firmly.

Step 5. Place ⅞" button over points of leaves. Push long doll needle threaded with heavy thread through button, both leaf points and entire pincushion until needle comes out bottom center. Pull slightly. Go back up through the apple, both leaves and button. Pull again enough to dimple the top and bottom of the apple to give it shape. Repeat several more times and tie off at the bottom. $

Autumn Breeze Sweatshirt Jacket

By Julie Weaver

Add the colors of autumn to a sale-priced sweatshirt, trim with flannel and you'll have a great gift or a treat for yourself.

Project Specifications

Skill Level: Beginner

Sweatshirt Size: Any Size

Note: Prewash sweatshirt and fabrics. Use ½" seams to prepare sweatshirt for appliqué.

Materials

- Autumn-colored sweatshirt
- 1 yard plaid flannel
- Plaid and striped flannel scraps for appliqué
- ¼ yard fusible interfacing
- Scraps of fusible transfer web
- All-purpose threads to match fabrics
- 6-strand embroidery floss to match appliqués
- Basic sewing supplies and tools

Instructions

Step 1. Cut bottom and neck ribbing from sweatshirt. Stay-stitch neck. Cut opening down center front. If you want to reduce bulk in your jacket, trim an equal amount from each side of the center front opening.

Step 2. Measure around bottom of sweatshirt, both sides of front opening and around the neck. Cut enough 4" bias strips from the plaid flannel to equal this measurement plus 18". Sew strips together end to end. Press the long sides wrong sides together. Pin raw edges to right side of jacket bottom, front and neck; stitch. Turn binding to the inside and slip-stitch in place.

Step 3. Cut sleeve ribbing from sweatshirt. Decide how long you want the sleeves to be, measure up from the cut edge and trim the sleeves at this point. Cut pocket from trimmed sleeve fabric.

Step 4. To make cuffs, measure the cut edge of sleeve and add 1". From plaid flannel cut two cuffs 8" by measurement. Cut two pieces of fusible interfacing 4" by measurement. Following manufacturer's instructions, fuse interfacing to one half of wrong side of each cuff. Press under ¼" on the other half of the cuff pieces. With right sides together, sew the side seam on each cuff.

Step 5. With right sides together, pin the cuff to the sleeve; stitch. Turn the cuff to the inside and slip-stitch in place over sewn seam. Turn cuff up on outside of jacket.

Step 6. Trace appliqué shapes on paper side of fusible transfer web. Cut out leaving roughly ½" around traced lines. Following manufacturer's instructions, fuse to selected fabrics.

Step 7. Referring to photo, position appliqués on front of jacket and center of pocket; fuse.

Step 8. With 3 strands of matching 6-strand embroidery floss, work buttonhole stitch around appliqué pieces. Work chain stitch on leaf vein, leaf stems, pumpkin curve lines and curlicue pump-kin tendrils as shown in Fig. 1.

Step 9. Place pocket and lining right sides together. Sew around pocket, leaving top open. Turn right side out and press. Cut a 6½" length of bias made in Step 2. Pin raw edges to top front of pocket, allowing ¼" overlap on each end. Stitch in place. Fold side edges in, turn binding to inside of pocket and slip-stitch in place. Attach pocket to front of jacket by hand or machine. $

Fig. 1
Chain Stitch

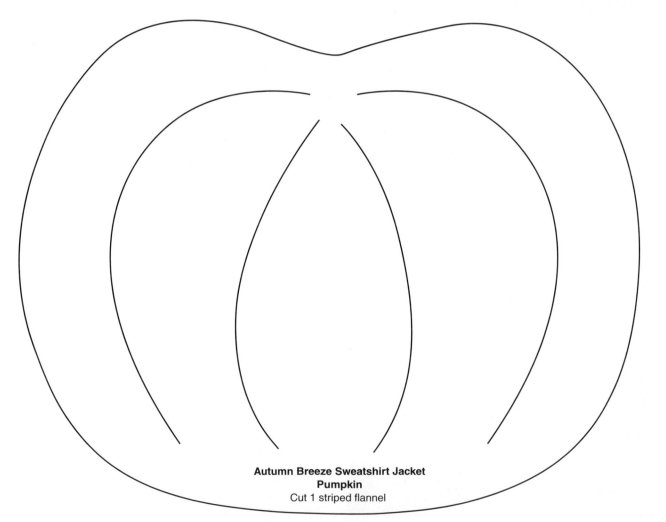

Autumn Breeze Sweatshirt Jacket
Pumpkin
Cut 1 striped flannel

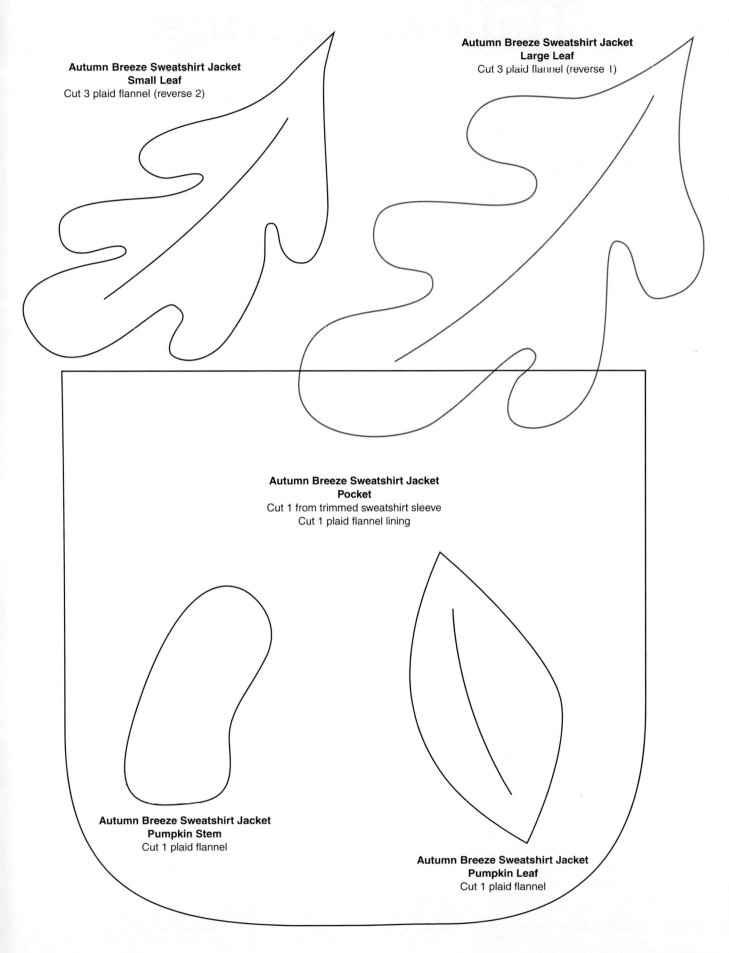

**Autumn Breeze Sweatshirt Jacket
Small Leaf**
Cut 3 plaid flannel (reverse 2)

**Autumn Breeze Sweatshirt Jacket
Large Leaf**
Cut 3 plaid flannel (reverse 1)

**Autumn Breeze Sweatshirt Jacket
Pocket**
Cut 1 from trimmed sweatshirt sleeve
Cut 1 plaid flannel lining

**Autumn Breeze Sweatshirt Jacket
Pumpkin Stem**
Cut 1 plaid flannel

**Autumn Breeze Sweatshirt Jacket
Pumpkin Leaf**
Cut 1 plaid flannel

Halloween Hugs

By Karen Mead

Witches are expected to be scary, but this one may charm you instead.
As a gift she will cast a spell on the lucky recipient.

Project Specifications

Skill Level: Beginner

Doll Size: Approximately 4" x 26"

Materials

- Fat quarter of black-and-tan checked fabric
- Scraps of black solid, muslin and orange plaid
- Muddy tan scraps for face
- Black and red acrylic paint
- Cosmetic blush
- Cotton swab
- 2 (⅜") black buttons
- Polyester fiberfill
- Bits of Spanish moss
- Paper witch hat
- ¼" paintbrush
- Several strands of raffia
- Craft glue
- All-purpose threads to match fabrics
- Basic sewing supplies and tools

Instructions

Step 1. Trace and cut all pieces as directed on patterns. From black-and-tan checked fabric cut two pieces 4" x 8" for body. Stitch one witch face piece to each body piece. Right sides together, stitch around head/body, leaving bottom open. Clip curves. Turn right side out and stuff firmly with polyester fiberfill.

Step 2. From black-and-tan checked fabric cut one piece 1¼" x 18". Fold in half lengthwise for arms and stitch 18" edge. Turn right side out. Tie a knot in the center for hands.

Step 3. From orange plaid cut four legs 2" x 13". Right sides facing, stitch two leg pieces together, rounding the foot as shown in Fig. 1. Leave top open. Turn right side out and stuff firmly with polyester fiberfill. Repeat for second leg.

Step 4. Insert legs in bottom of body.

Fig. 1
Round end of leg
for foot as shown.

Turn in raw edges of body and stitch legs in place.

Step 5. From black-and-tan checked fabric cut a skirt piece 10" x 20". Right sides together, bring 10" ends together and stitch. Run a gathering stitch along one long edge. Draw up threads, place on witch body and stitch in place to secure.

Step 6. Stitch arm ends together, then stitch in place at center back where head and body meet.

Step 7. Stitch buttons on dress front, leaving knot showing on front of buttons.

Step 8. Stitch nose pieces together with ⅛" seam, leaving open on wide end. Turn right side out and turn under open edges. Sew to face with invisible stitches.

Step 9. Referring to photo, paint shoe at end of leg with black acrylic paint.

Step 10. Right sides together, sew ghost, bat and pumpkin with ⅛" seam, leaving 1" opening in each. Clip curves, turn right side out and stuff lightly with polyester fiberfill. Close openings with hand stitches.

Step 11. Dip handle of paintbrush in black acrylic paint and dot eyes and three buttons on ghost front and eyes and warts

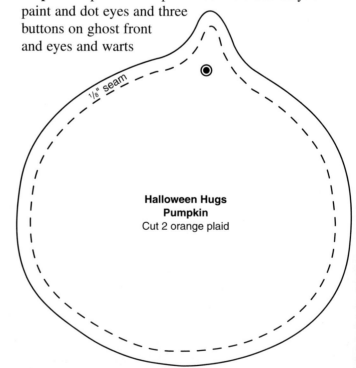

⅛" seam

**Halloween Hugs
Pumpkin**
Cut 2 orange plaid

on witch face. With red acrylic paint, add a tiny heart-shaped mouth to witch face and apply cosmetic blush to cheeks with cotton swab.

Step 12. Glue pumpkin, ghost and bat under witch's arms. Tie a raffia bow and glue to pumpkin stem.

Step 13. Glue hat to witch head. Glue a bit of polyester fiberfill under hat brim for hair. Glue strands of Spanish moss to top of hat brim. $

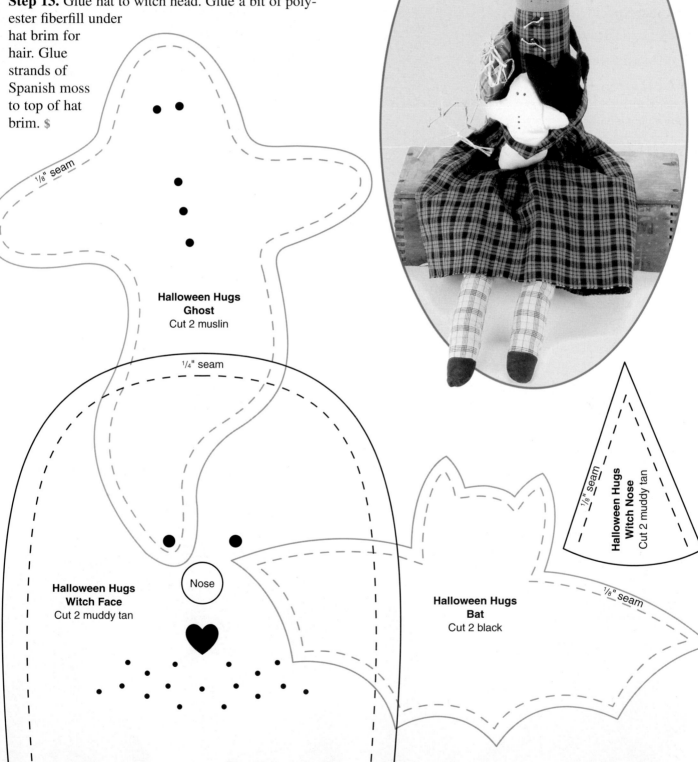

¹/₈" seam

**Halloween Hugs
Ghost**
Cut 2 muslin

¹/₄" seam

**Halloween Hugs
Witch Face**
Cut 2 muddy tan

Nose

**Halloween Hugs
Bat**
Cut 2 black

¹/₈" seam

¹/₈" seam

**Halloween Hugs
Witch Nose**
Cut 2 muddy tan

¹/₈" seam

Falling Leaves Pot Holders

By Mary Ayres

*A nice little gift—perfect for many occasions. It requires only
a little time and a few scraps from your fabric stash.*

Project Specifications

Skill Level: Beginner

Pot Holder Size: Approximately 7" x 7"

*Note: Materials are for two pot holders. Fabrics and
batting should be 100 percent cotton. Man-made fibers
may melt with heat.*

Materials

- Scraps of tan solid for front square and
backing
- Scraps of cream solid for word strips
- Scraps of homespun for strips
- Scraps of gold and rust for appliqué
- 6-strand embroidery floss in black and colors
that match appliqués
- Scraps of fusible transfer web
- 1¾ yards black piping
- 8" piece of black double-fold bias tape
- 4 squares flat cotton batting 7½" x 7½"
- Basic sewing supplies and tools

Instructions

Step 1. From tan solid fabric cut one square 5½" x
5½". Cut a strip 1½" x 6½" from cream solid fabric.
From three different homespuns cut one strip 1½" x
5½", 1½" x 6½" and 1½" x 7½".

Step 2. Sew 5½" homespun strip to left side of tan
square. Press seam allowance toward strip. Sew cream
strip to bottom of square; press seam allowance

toward square. Sew 6½" strip to left side of square;
press toward outer strip. Sew 7½" strip to bottom of
block; press toward outer strip.

Step 3. Repeat Steps 1 and 2 for second square.

Step 4. Trace each leaf pattern on paper side of fusible
transfer web as instructed on pattern. Cut out leaving
roughly ½" around each traced line.

Step 5. Following manufacturer's instructions, fuse to

selected fabrics.
Cut out on
traced lines.
Referring to
photo for
placement,
fuse leaves to
pieced squares.

Step 6.
Transfer
remaining
details of leaves and
words to cream word
strips. Work buttonhole
stitch around each
leaf with 3 strands
of matching
embroidery floss.
Embroider stem
stitch on words and leaf detail
with 2 strands of black
embroidery floss.

Step 7. Baste
two batting
squares to back
of each pieced
square. Sew pip-
ing around front
of each pot hold-
er ¼" from the
edge, beginning
and ending in top
right corner. Clip pip-
ing seam at corners
as you work
around square.

Step 8. Cut double-fold
bias tape into two 4" strips.
Sew each strip close to folded
edges. Bring short ends together
and baste one hanging loop to top
right corner of each pot holder front,
matching raw edges.

Step 9. From tan solid fabric cut two backing squares
7½" x 7½". Right sides together, sew a back to each
front, leaving a 4" opening along one side. Trim corners and turn right side out. Close opening with hand
stitches. $

Falling Leaves Pot Holders
Maple Leaf
Cut 1 rust

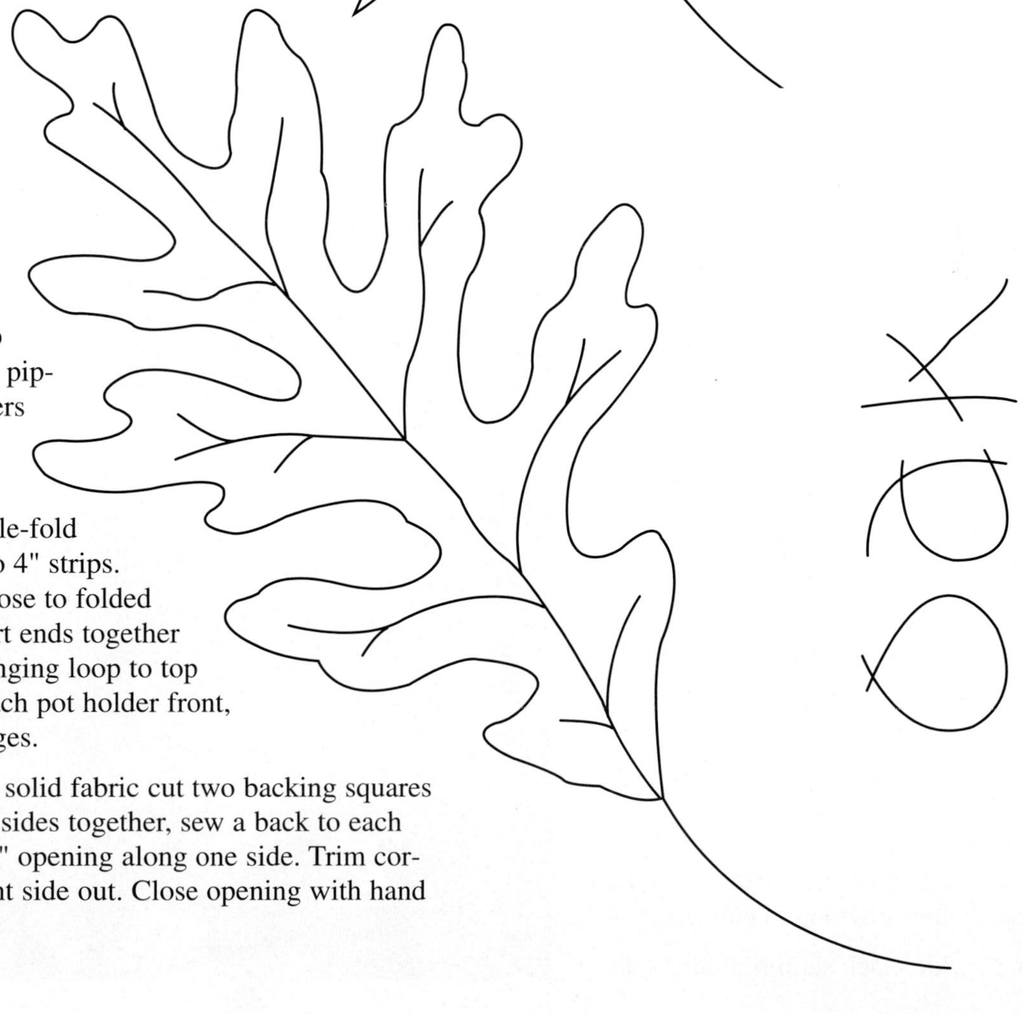

Falling Leaves Pot Holders
Oak Leaf
Cut 1 gold

Friendly Frankie Trick-or-Treat Bag

By Mary Ayres

These bags are so quick and easy you can make one for every kid on the block!

Project Specifications

Skill Level: Beginner

Bag Size: Approximately 8" x 10"

Materials

- 2 pieces orange felt 8½" x 11"
- Scraps of gold and purple felt
- 2 strips dark green burlap 1¾" x 8¼"
- Light green burlap 8½" x 8½"
- 2 (¾") black flat buttons
- 19" (1"-wide) black satin ribbon
- Black, orange and white 6-strand embroidery floss
- Black all-purpose sewing thread
- Basic sewing supplies and tools

Instructions

Step 1. Cut bag and face shapes as instructed on pattern.

Step 2. Pin green burlap face to one orange bag shape. With black thread sew along top of face ¼" from edge. Pull threads above stitching line to fringe burlap.

Step 3. Cut nose and cheeks as instructed on patterns. Pin to face as indicated. Work button-hole stitch around cheeks with 6 strands of white embroidery floss and around nose with 6 strands of orange embroidery floss.

Step 4. Transfer mouth to face. With 6 strands of black embroidery floss, embroider mouth with stem stitch. Sew black buttons to face for eyes with white embroidery floss.

Step 5. With black all-purpose sewing thread, stitch dark green burlap strip to wrong side of each orange felt bag piece with ½" seam. Fold over to front of bag and sew ¼" from edge. Pull burlap threads below stitching line to fringe.

Step 6. Cut 1"-wide black satin ribbon in half to make two 9½" pieces. Pin ribbons to top wrong side of bag front and back for handles. Place each end 1¾" from sides of bag with ¾" of ends inside bag. Attach to bag by sewing a rectangle with an X in the middle on the bag front side.

Step 7. Sew bag front to bag back ¼" from edge, wrong sides together. Pull burlap threads around outside of face stitching to fringe. $

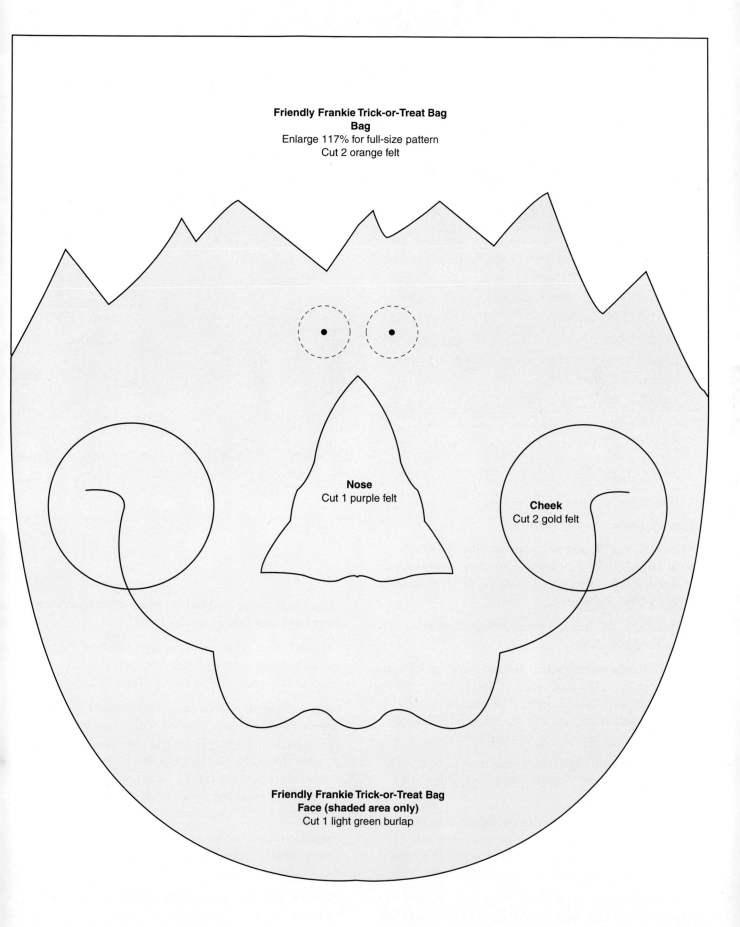

Friendly Frankie Trick-or-Treat Bag
Bag
Enlarge 117% for full-size pattern
Cut 2 orange felt

Nose
Cut 1 purple felt

Cheek
Cut 2 gold felt

Friendly Frankie Trick-or-Treat Bag
Face (shaded area only)
Cut 1 light green burlap

Miss Witch

By Mary Ayres

Everyone loves to celebrate holidays by wearing an appropriate symbol.
What could be more fun for Halloween than a green witch with orange hair?

Project Specifications

Skill Level: Beginner

Pin Size: Approximately 3½" x 3½"

Materials

- 3¾" and 1" circles of green solid fabric for face and nose
- 2½" x 8½" strip of black burlap for hat
- 1½" black felt circle
- 2 (5mm) black beads
- Black and lime-green 6-strand embroidery floss
- Orange craft hair
- ⅜ yard ½"-wide purple ribbon
- 3" straw broom
- Polyester fiberfill
- 1½" gold pin fastener
- Fabric glue
- Basic sewing supplies and tools

Instructions

Step 1. Run a basting stitch around the 3¾" green solid fabric circle. Pull basting stitches tightly to gather, leaving a 1" opening. Stuff circle firmly with polyester fiberfill and flatten.

Step 2. Sew 1½" black felt circle to back of head, covering circle opening.

Step 3. Run a basting stitch around the 1" green solid fabric circle. Roll a tiny piece of polyester fiberfill into a ball and place inside circle. Pull basting stitches tightly to gather and knot to secure. Using invisible stitches, sew gathered side of nose to face.

Step 4. Going through entire thickness of head, sew black beads to face ⅛" above nose and with ⅛" of space between eyes.

Step 5. Going through entire thickness of head, embroider a French knot wart on lower left side of nose, using 3 strands of lime-green embroidery floss and wrapping floss three times around needle.

Step 6. Referring to photo for placement, draw a wiggly mouth on face with pencil. Embroider mouth with stem stitch, using 2 strands of black embroidery floss. Begin and end floss in back of head.

Step 7. Cut an 8" piece of orange craft hair. Place it across top and sides of head. Sew hair to center top of head and on each side to secure. Trim hair ends.

Step 8. Bring short ends of 2½" x 8½" black burlap strip together and sew with ¼" seam. This seam will be the center back of the hat. Turn right side out. Sew basting stitches around hat ½" from top and ¾" from bottom. Gather stitches at top tightly and knot. Gather stitches at bottom to fit head and knot. Stitch hat to head in several places to secure. Fringe bottom ends of hat.

Step 9. Stitch 3" straw broom to hat at an angle. Wrap purple ribbon around hat and broom and tie at center front. Stitch to secure.

Step 10. Sew 1½" gold pin fastener to center back of hat. $

"Boy ... Am I Stuffed" Wall Hanging

By Chris Malone

This Thanksgiving special can probably be constructed from scraps in your stash.
Even the back can be pieced if you'd like to economize to the max!

Project Specifications

Skill Level: Beginner

Wall Quilt Size: 13" x 13"

Materials

- Square of muslin 10½" x 10½"
- ⅛ yard of rust print fabric
- 2 strips each 2½" x 9½" and 2½" x 13½" gold-and-cream checked fabric
- Scraps of print and solid gold and rust, and white-on-white print
- Black 6-strand embroidery floss
- Scraps of fusible transfer web
- Batting 17½" x 17½"
- Backing 17½" x 17½"
- Rust and natural quilting thread
- 2 (3mm) black beads
- 3 (1¹⁄₁₆") gold buttons
- 1" x 16" wooden slat
- 2 (1¼") wooden half-balls
- Cream and gold acrylic paints
- Satin varnish
- 2 small sawtooth hangers
- Air- or water-soluble marker
- Small paintbrush
- Craft glue
- Basic sewing supplies and tools

Instructions

Step 1. With pencil, mark an 8½" square within 10½" muslin square. With air- or water-soluble marker, trace the words located under the turkey pattern. Bottom of "B" should be 1⅛" above bottom pencil line and ⅞" from left side line. Tape pattern and fabric to a window to facilitate tracing.

Step 2. With 2 strands of 6-strand black embroidery floss, backstitch letters and make French knots for dots.

Step 3. Trace appliqué pieces on paper side of fusible transfer web. Cut out leaving approximately ½" margin around traced lines. Refer to photo for fabric suggestions and fuse shapes to selected fabrics following manufacturer's instructions.

Step 4. Cut out shapes on traced lines and arrange on muslin square; fuse.

Step 5. With 1 strand of black embroidery floss, back-stitch mouth and make French knot at each end of smile. Stitch straight lines for eyebrows.

Step 6. Trim muslin to marked 8½" square. From rust print cut two strips each 1" x 8½" and 1" x 9½". Sew shorter strips to top and bottom of square and longer strips to sides. Press seam allowances toward border.

Step 7. Sew shorter gold checked fabric strips to top and bottom of square and longer strips to sides. Press seam allowances toward gold border.

Step 8. Place backing right side up on working surface. Place appliquéd square, right side down, over backing, and place batting on top. Smooth all layers and pin to secure. Cut backing and batting even with appliquéd square.

Step 9. Sew around all edges, leaving a 5" opening at bottom center. Trim batting close to seam and trim corners. Turn right side out and close opening with hand stitches.

Step 10. Baste or pin through center of each border. With matching quilting thread, quilt in the ditch by hand or machine along outer edge of block and along border seams.

Step 11. From rust print fabric cut three rectangles 3" x 6½" for hanging loops. Fold each in half lengthwise, right sides together, and sew around all raw edges leaving a 2" opening. Clip corners and turn right side out. Close opening with hand stitches.

Step 12. Fold one loop over top center of quilt, over-lapping ends 1" on front and back. Sew gold button on

Boy... am I stuffed.

**"Boy ... Am I Stuffed" Wall Hanging
Turkey and Words**

loop end on front of quilt, sewing through all layers. Position and sew remaining loops 2" from each end.

Step 13. Referring to pattern for placement, sew black beads in place for eyes.

Step 14. Paint wooden slat cream and half-balls gold.

Apply second coat if necessary. Finish with one coat of satin varnish.

Step 15. Attach sawtooth hangers to ends of slat and glue half-balls to other side of ends. Slip loops over slat to hang. $

Mosaic Leaves Basket Topper

By Janna Britton

Use little snippets of autumn-colored fabrics to create a multicolored pattern on the leaves decorating this useful covered basket.

Project Specifications

Skill Level: Beginner

Basket Size: 12" x 11" x 5½"

Note: Instructions may be varied for any basket size.

Materials

- Chipwood basket 12" x 11" x 5½"
- White mat board 12" x 12"
- Muslin 12" x 24"
- Assorted 2" x 6" fabric scraps in autumn colors: brown, yellow, orange, green and burgundy
- Burgundy, gold, and brown felt squares
- Cotton batting 14" x 14"
- 1¼ yards (1¼"-wide) ecru gathered eyelet lace
- 1¼ yards burgundy bias tape
- 2 yards (1½"-wide) burgundy grosgrain ribbon
- 1½ yards fusible transfer web
- Gold pearl dimensional paint
- Gold metallic acrylic paint
- Gold acorn/leaf ornament
- Old toothbrush
- Plastic lid or receptacle for paint
- Straightedge
- Pinking shears
- Craft knife
- Fabric glue
- Low-temperature glue gun
- Basic sewing supplies and tools

Instructions

Step 1. Trace basket top on mat board and cut out with craft knife.

Step 2. Measure handle width and cut that width from center of mat board piece. This will make three pieces: left side, center and right side. Check center placement and size. It may need to be trimmed shorter to fit within handle edges.

Step 3. Trace each mat piece on paper side of fusible transfer web. Cut out leaving roughly ¼" margin around traced lines. Following manufacturer's instructions, fuse to cotton batting. Cut out on traced lines. Arrange each of the three mat board pieces on work surface and fuse batting separately to each.

Step 4. Fold muslin in half to make a 12" x 12" square. Place pieces adjacent to each other, batting side down, on muslin. Trace around each piece with pencil. Stitch around perimeter ⅛" outside traced line, leaving one side open. Turn right side out and stitch ⅛" outside two center lines.

Step 5. Insert lid pieces, batting side up, into muslin pockets. Close opening with hand stitches.

Step 6. Make a small puddle of gold metallic acrylic paint on plastic lid or other receptacle. Dampen old toothbrush with water. Place basket top on protected work surface and spatter-paint gold onto muslin by running a straightedge across toothbrush. Allow to dry.

Step 7. Place basket top on top of basket. Beginning at one handle edge and using fabric glue, attach ecru eyelet lace around top edge of muslin, wrapping around outer edge of basket handle. Place bias tape on top of ruffle and glue. Turn under at end and secure with glue.

Step 8. Cut grosgrain ribbon in half. Wrap each around a handle end and tie in bows. Trim ends in inverted V. Attach acorn/leaf ornament to center of one bow with low-temperature glue gun.

Step 9. With pinking shears cut leaves as directed on patterns.

Step 10. Following manufacturer's instructions, fuse transfer web to assorted autumn-colored fabric scraps. Cut many small leaf-shaped snippets from each fabric as shown in Fig. 1. Let pieces of

Fig. 1
Cut small snippets with curved edges at random as shown.

many colors fall randomly on each felt leaf until totally covered to within ⅛" of edges; fuse.

Step 11. Arrange leaves on basket top. Use low-temperature glue gun to glue in place.

Step 12. Use gold pearl dimensional paint to add highlights to leaves and to make small loopy tendrils between leaves. Refer to photo for placement. $

Pattern continued on page 131

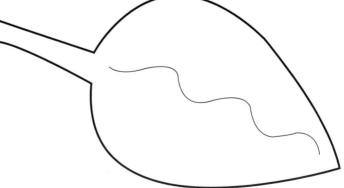

Mosaic Leaves Basket Topper
Small Leaf
Cut 2 gold, 1 brown & 1 burgundy felt

Pumpkin-Patch Car Coat

By June Fiechter

*This seasonal denim topper will send a little girl off
to school happy and comfortable on a crisp autumn day.*

Project Specifications

Skill Level: Beginner

Coat Size: Children's 7-8-10

*Designer note: The economy of this coat is achieved from
the use of recycled fabric. I used a denim dress for the
coat, and green and orange shirts for collar and appliqué.*

Materials

- McCalls pattern 2403
- New or recycled fabric as designated on pattern (unlined)
- Scraps of new or recycled orange, green, brown and light green for appliqué
- 3 (⅝") navy buttons
- 1 yard jute or twine
- ¼ yard fusible transfer web
- Machine-appliqué threads to match or contrast with appliqué pieces
- All-purpose navy sewing thread
- Basic sewing supplies and tools

Instructions

Step 1. Cut out coat as directed on pattern. Cut coat from denim, collar from green fabric and cuffs from orange. To limit the amount of denim required, eliminate the portion of the pattern below the solid line that reads: "To shorten, fold on this line." There are two such lines. Eliminate below the one nearest the hem at the bottom.

Step 2. Trace appliqué pieces on paper side of fusible transfer web as indicated on patterns. Cut out leaving roughly ½" margin around traced lines.

Step 3. Following manufacturer's instructions, fuse appliqué pieces to selected fabrics. Cut out on traced lines. Referring to photo, arrange pieces on coat front pieces and fuse in place.

Step 4. With matching or contrasting thread, machine-appliqué around pieces and center veins of leaves. Straight-stitch secondary veins of leaves and curve lines of pumpkins. Work white highlight areas by zigzagging over area. Start with narrow stitch, increase width at center and gradually reduce width again.

Step 5. Arrange twine or jute in curlicue tendril from pumpkin stems. Zigzag over the tendril to secure.

Step 6. Continue construction of coat as instructed on pattern. Place twine or jute ¼" from edge of collar. Zigzag over the twine to secure.

Step 7. With navy thread, stitch several curved lines across front of coat as shown in Figure 1. This will hold the front facing in place and create the illusion of the leaf floating in the breeze. $

**Pumpkin-Patch Car Coat
Leaf**
Cut 4 green (reverse 2)

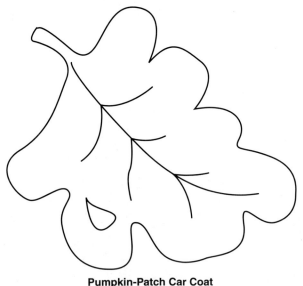

**Pumpkin-Patch Car Coat
Oak Leaf**
Cut 2 green (reverse 1)

128 • *Sew Creative Gifts for Under $10*

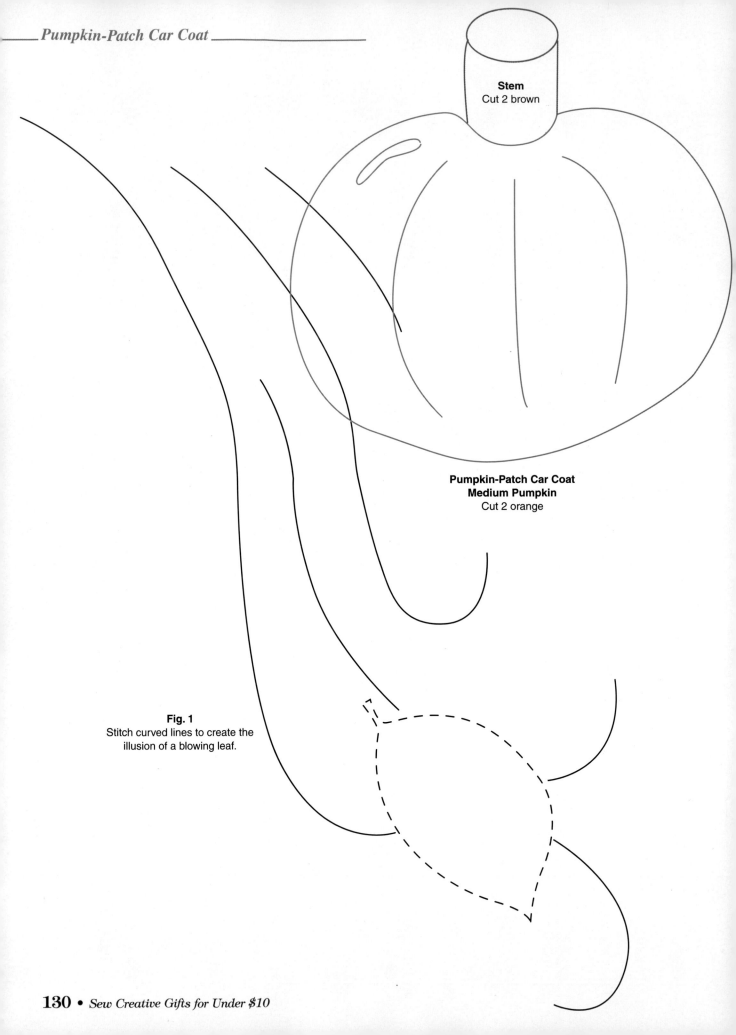

Stem
Cut 2 brown

Pumpkin-Patch Car Coat
Medium Pumpkin
Cut 2 orange

Fig. 1
Stitch curved lines to create the
illusion of a blowing leaf.

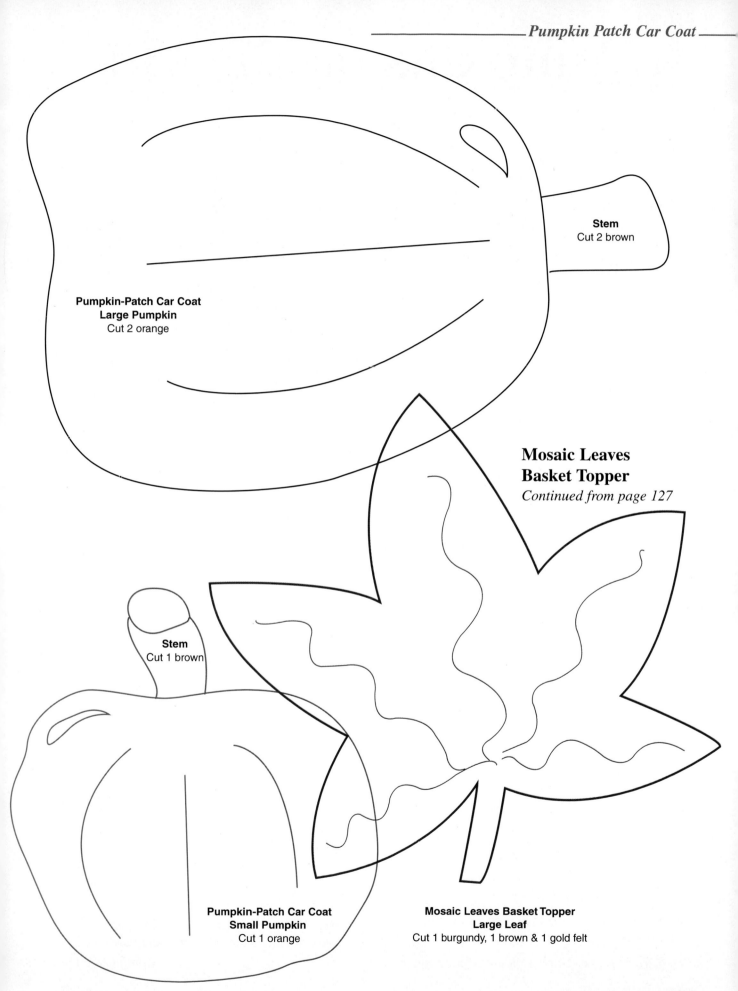

Stem
Cut 2 brown

**Pumpkin-Patch Car Coat
Large Pumpkin**
Cut 2 orange

Mosaic Leaves
Basket Topper
Continued from page 127

Stem
Cut 1 brown

**Pumpkin-Patch Car Coat
Small Pumpkin**
Cut 1 orange

**Mosaic Leaves Basket Topper
Large Leaf**
Cut 1 burgundy, 1 brown & 1 gold felt

Pumpkins on the Vine

By Debbie Roney

These mini-pumpkins involve mini-work and mini-materials. Not only are they great "on the vine," but they also cluster nicely for refrigerator magnets, box tops and hair clips.

Project Specifications

Skill Level: Beginner

Necklace Size: Any size

Designer Note: *All autumn colors work well, even dark green with lighter green beads and leaves. For brighter orange pumpkins use orange yarn for stuffing to enhance the orange color.*

Materials

- Scraps of a variety of orange and peach fabrics for pumpkins
- Scraps of green small-leaf print fabric for leaves
- White yarn for stuffing
- All-purpose sewing threads to match fabrics
- Fray Check or clear-drying glue
- 6-strand embroidery floss or pearl cotton for stringing necklace
- Large needle for stringing pumpkins
- Sharp-pointed scissors
- Basic sewing supplies and tools

Instructions

Step 1. Put Fray Check or clear-drying glue on five small leaves printed on green small-leaf print. Select leaves far enough apart to be cut out separately. Dry and carefully cut out leaves.

Step 2. Trace pumpkin shape on the reverse side of five various orange or peach fabrics. Do not cut out. Fold fabric, right sides together, and sew on traced lines. Leave ½" opening at top. Carefully secure stopping and starting places. Cut out, leaving ¼" seam allowance.

Step 3. Turn pumpkins right side out and stuff with bits of yarn. The pumpkins should remain flat, so do not over-stuff. Close openings with hand stitches.

Step 4. Using matching or contrasting threads, quilt two or three ribs on each pumpkin.

Step 5. Tack one leaf made in Step 1 to top of each pumpkin.

Step 6. Trace six bead circles on green-leaf print, leaving

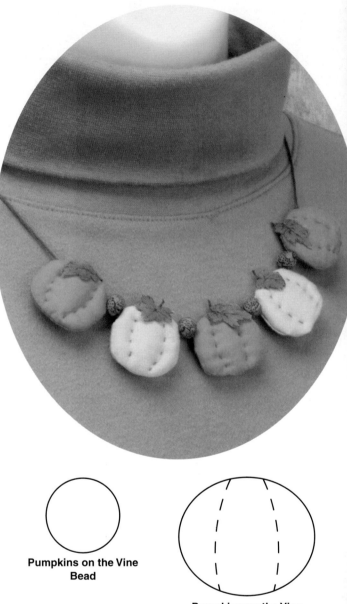

Pumpkins on the Vine Bead

Pumpkins on the Vine Pumpkin

at least ½" between circles. Cut ¼" outside traced line. With needle and double thread, work a running stitch on traced line. Draw up thread, tucking seam allowance to inside of bead for stuffing.

Step 7. Measure a length of embroidery floss or pearl cotton for stringing pumpkins and beads. Add 4" to

Continued on page 135

Johnny's Apple Trail

By Janna Britton

*Because felt is so easy to work with and comes in such yummy colors,
you'll love making and giving this harvest table runner.*

Project Specifications

Skill Level: Beginner

Table Runner Size: 35½" x 13¾"

Materials

- Butterscotch felt 34½" x 11½"
- Ruby red felt 35½" x 13¾"
- 2 squares cranberry red felt
- 1 square leaf green felt
- 1 square off-white felt
- 1 square brown felt
- Fusible transfer web 33½" x 10½"
- Leaf green, cranberry red, brown and off-white 6-strand embroidery floss to match felt
- Pinking shears or pinking-blade rotary cutter
- 1 package green rickrack to match green felt
- Basic sewing supplies and tools

Instructions

Step 1. Cut appliqué pieces as directed on patterns.

Step 2. Cut edges of butterscotch felt with pinking shears or pinking-blade rotary cutter.

Step 3. Referring to photo, arrange green rickrack in pattern as shown. Stitch in place with 3 strands of green embroidery floss and a straight running stitch.

Step 4. Place appliqué pieces as shown in photo. Sewing through butterscotch panel, work buttonhole stitch around apples, curved edges of apple slices, apple core bases and tops with 3 strands of cranberry red embroidery floss. Stitch straight edges of apple slices and apple cores with 3 strands of off-white floss and a straight running stitch.

Step 5. Stitch stems in place with 3 strands of brown floss and a straight running stitch. With 3 strands of green floss work fly stitch on leaves as shown in Fig. 1.

Step 6. Lazy-daisy stitch each seed in place with 3 strands of brown floss as shown on page 173.

Step 7. Following manufacturer's directions, fuse butterscotch panel to ruby-red panel. With 3 strands of cranberry red floss, work a running stitch ¼" from edges of butterscotch panel through both layers of felt. $

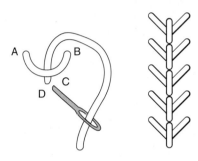

Fig. 1
Fly Stitch

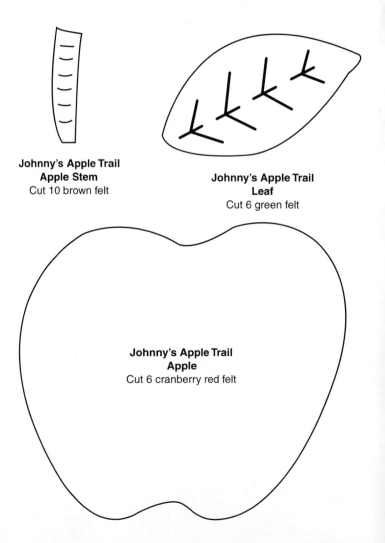

**Johnny's Apple Trail
Apple Stem**
Cut 10 brown felt

**Johnny's Apple Trail
Leaf**
Cut 6 green felt

**Johnny's Apple Trail
Apple**
Cut 6 cranberry red felt

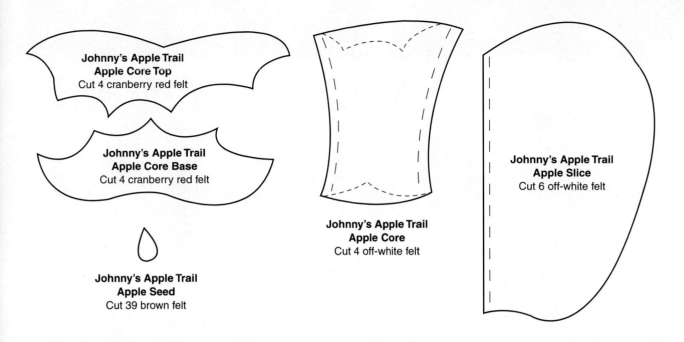

**Johnny's Apple Trail
Apple Core Top**
Cut 4 cranberry red felt

**Johnny's Apple Trail
Apple Core Base**
Cut 4 cranberry red felt

**Johnny's Apple Trail
Apple Seed**
Cut 39 brown felt

**Johnny's Apple Trail
Apple Core**
Cut 4 off-white felt

**Johnny's Apple Trail
Apple Slice**
Cut 6 off-white felt

Pumpkins on the Vine

Continued from page 132

the length for ties. Find the center of the stringing thread. Measure out 3" and tie a knot. Thread the large needle on the other end of the thread and string one pumpkin, stopping at the knot. Alternate beads and pumpkins for a total of five pumpkins and four beads. Tie another knot.

Step 8. Check for proper hanging length and tie ends. Thread a bead at the end of each tie as shown in Fig. 1. $

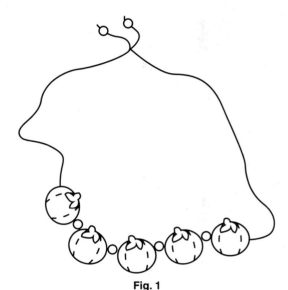

Fig. 1
Thread a bead at end of each tie.

Winterfest

Winterfest holidays include anything from Christmas and the New Year to the season's first snow. Celebrate them with festive projects for one and all!

Stitch up the Festive Holiday Basket and then fill it with Berry Christmas Towels. Give one to each guest who visits your home during the holiday season. Stitch a Wishful Snowman Stocking and fill it with gifts for a lucky grandchild. Or sew with love an Old World Santa—sure to be displayed with pride year after year!

None of these gifts will break your budget, so make several for everyone on your gift list! And be sure to stitch one (or several) for yourself while you're at it!

Festive Holiday Basket

By Janna Britton

Fill this trimmed basket with pinecones, homemade cookies, snack mix or gourmet condiments.

Project Specifications

Skill Level: Beginner

Basket Size: Approximately 11" x 8" x 5"

Note: Lining can be easily adjusted for other basket sizes.

Materials

- Basket 11" x 8" x 5"
- ⅜ yard Christmas fabric
- All-purpose threads to match fabrics
- 2 yards (¾"-wide) lace threaded with satin ribbon
- 6 wooden heart shapes—2 small, 2 medium and 2 large
- 2 wooden teardrop shapes for tree trunks
- 2 (½") red heart buttons
- Low-temperature glue and glue gun
- Green acrylic paint
- Glitter 3-D icicle paint
- ½" flat paintbrush
- Basic sewing supplies and tools

Instructions

Step 1. Measure around outside of top basket rim and

add 1". From Christmas fabric cut lining piece that measurement by 3".

Step 2. Turn raw edge under ¼" on two short ends and one long edge and stitch.

Step 3. From Christmas fabric cut two ruffle pieces 5" x 42". (To adjust ruffle size for other-size basket, cut twice as long as basket liner.)

Step 4. Fold ruffle pieces in half lengthwise, right sides together. Stitch short ends with ¼" seam allowance. Turn right side out and align raw edges. Run a gathering stitch through both layers ¼" from raw edge. Gather threads to make ruffle.

Step 5. Right sides together, raw edges aligned, pin ruffle pieces evenly gathered on liner piece; stitch with ¼" seam allowance.

Step 6. Glue one end of lace threaded with satin ribbon to inner handle edge. Wrap around and around the handle and glue to inner side of other handle edge. Cut off excess lace.

Step 7. Insert liner into basket with ruffle openings at handles. Glue ruffle seam along top edge of basket. Glue liner to inside of basket, carefully smoothing in place.

Step 8. Glue three wooden heart shapes together as shown in Fig. 1. Glue teardrop point under center of largest heart for tree trunk. Repeat for two trees.

Step 9. Paint trees with green acrylic paint. Repeat when dry if necessary to cover completely. Paint small decorative curves on tree with glitter 3-D icicle paint. When dry, glue red heart buttons to tops of trees.

Step 10. From lace threaded with satin ribbon, cut two 16" pieces. Tie a bow with each piece. Glue bows to basket handles and glue trees to center of bows. $

Fig. 1
Glue 3 heart shapes together & add teardrop as shown.

Berry Christmas Towel

By Mary Ayres

Buy a number of textured off-white towels at your craft or fabric store, add a few scraps and stitches, and you can quickly make holiday towels you'll be proud to give.

Project Specifications

Skill Level: Beginner

Towel Size: Any size

Materials

- Off-white textured towel
- Red and green fabric scraps
- Scraps of fusible transfer web
- Red, green, black and white 6-strand embroidery floss
- Basic sewing supplies and tools

Instructions

Step 1. Trace appliqué patterns on paper side of fusible transfer web as directed on patterns. Cut out leaving roughly ½" margin around traced lines. Following manufacturer's instructions, fuse to selected fabrics.

Step 2. Referring to photo for placement, arrange appliqués on towel; fuse.

Step 3. Transfer words and leaf veins to towel. With 3 strands of black embroidery floss, work buttonhole stitch around shapes and along leaf veins.

Step 4. With 3 strands of red embroidery floss, work stem stitch on word "berry"; with 3 strands of green floss embroider "christmas."

Step 5. With 3 strands of white embroidery floss, make a French knot at upper right side of berry as indicated on pattern. Wrap floss around needle three times.

Step 6. With 3 strands of black embroidery floss, work buttonhole stitch along lower front edge of towel. $

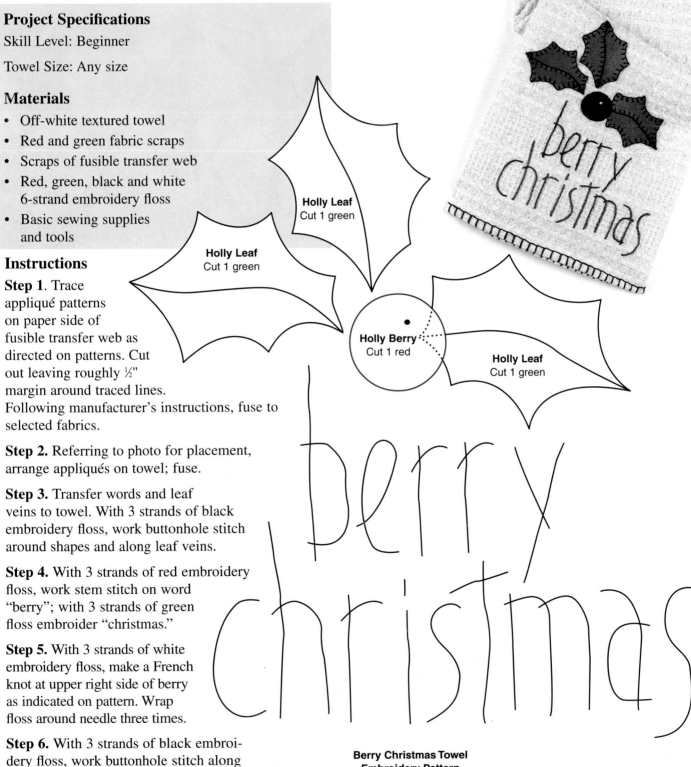

Holly Leaf
Cut 1 green

Holly Leaf
Cut 1 green

Holly Berry
Cut 1 red

Holly Leaf
Cut 1 green

**Berry Christmas Towel
Embroidery Pattern**

Kountry Kris Kringle

By Chris Malone

Make it a point to look for recycled materials to minimize the cost of this great Santa figure. Recycled flannel shirts and sheets can be cut for fabric, and shopping garage and estate sales will rapidly expand your button collection.

Project Specifications

Skill Level: Beginner

Kris Kringle Size: Approximately 7" x 16"

Materials

- Unbleached muslin 12" x 10"
- Black solid fabric 10" x 7"
- ⅓ yard or fat quarter of red checked flannel
- 1½" x 18" strip green plaid flannel
- White or tan shaggy plush felt, sherpa or fake fur 1" x 37½" and 1½" x 1½" for trim
- Cotton batting or felt 6" x 8"
- Black 6-strand embroidery floss
- 1 (⅜") rounded shank button for nose
- 2 (³⁄₁₆") black buttons for eyes
- 3 (⅝") red buttons for tree
- 1 (1") black button for belt trim
- 2 gold, 1 red and 1 green (⅞"–1") buttons
- 8" (⅜"-diameter) tree branch
- 3" grapevine wreath
- 36" (20-gauge) black or rusty wire
- Polyester fiberfill
- Pink cosmetic blush
- Cotton swab
- 1 (¾") plastic ring for hanger
- White marker
- Hot-glue gun
- Wire cutters
- Basic sewing supplies and tools

Instructions

Step 1. Fold muslin in half. Trace head/body on one side of doubled fabric. Pin fabric to hold layers securely and sew on traced lines, leaving bottom open. Cut out ⅛" from seam; clip curves and turn right side out. Stuff firmly with polyester fiberfill.

Step 2. In same manner, fold black solid fabric in half and trace two legs and two arms with white marker.

Sew on traced lines, leaving open at short straight ends. Cut out, clip curves and turn right side out.

Step 3. Stuff each arm firmly with polyester fiberfill. Turn in ¼" on raw edges and close opening with hand stitches. Stitch across middle of each arm, where indicated by dashed line on pattern, so arm will bend easily. Slip-stitch each arm to shoulder, as indicated by dots on pattern, with thumbs facing up.

Step 4. Stuff each leg firmly and baste top of each leg together ¼" from raw edge. Insert top of legs into body opening, toes pointing out. Close opening with hand stitches, catching legs in seam.

Step 5. Trace and cut nose circle from muslin. Cut shank off of ⅜" rounded shank button with wire cutters. Hand-sew gathering stitches around edge of muslin circle. Place a small piece of fiberfill in center of circle, then button, rounded side down, on fiberfill. Pull gathering thread tightly to cover button; knot and clip thread. Glue nose, gathered side down, to face.

Step 6. Sew ³⁄₁₆" black buttons to face for eyes. Use cotton swab to apply blush to cheeks and top of nose.

Step 7. Trace and cut suit and hat pieces as instructed on pattern. Pin suit front and back, right sides together, and sew a ¼" seam, leaving open at neck, sleeve ends and bottom. Clip underarm and turn right side out. Press raw edges of neck in ¼".

Step 8. Slip suit over Santa's head and insert arms into sleeves. Hand-sew gathering stitches at end of each sleeve; pull thread to gather snugly at wrist. Repeat for bottom of suit. Gather-stitch neck edge, but pull thread only enough to gather gently around neck.

Step 9. Pin hat front and back, right sides together, and sew ¼" seam, leaving open at bottom. Trim tip and turn right side out. Hand-sew gathering stitches at bottom of hat. Hold a small piece of fiberfill on top of head and slip hat onto head. Pull gathering thread enough to fit hat to head.

Step 10. From 1" x 37½" fur trim strip, cut a 6" length for suit bottom, 5" strip for neck, 6¼" strip for hat,

13¼" strip for waist and two 3½" lengths for sleeves. Glue each strip in place, overlapping ends slightly in back and gluing or whipstitching overlapped edges together. Overlap ends of sleeve trim in front so when arms are bent inward ends will not show.

Step 11. Glue 1" black button to center front of waist trim.

Step 12. Use hat-ball pattern to cut circle from 1½" x 1½" square fur trim fabric. Hand-sew gathering stitches around edge of circle. Insert polyester fiberfill in center of circle and pull stitches tight to form a ball. Glue ball to front of hat tip, gathered side down. Referring to photo, fold hat at an angle and use glue to hold in place.

Step 13. Cut mustache and beard pieces as directed on patterns. Using 2 strands of black embroidery floss, sew beard front and back together with a running stitch ³⁄₁₆" from edge. Repeat for two mustache pairs. Glue top of beard to face and mustache directly under nose.

Step 14. Cut green flannel strip into three equal pieces. Tie each strip around tree branch with first strip ¾" from end of branch and ½" between strips. Trim each side evenly. Glue one ⅝" red button over each knot and a ⅞"–1" gold button to top of branch. Position branch on one side of body. Tack branch to Santa, sewing through suit and into body. Bend arm forward and glue hand over branch, covering stitches.

Step 15. Cut 20-gauge wire in half. Wrap one piece around the grapevine wreath two times to secure. Push one end of wire through holes of one remaining button and around wreath. Repeat to attach two more buttons. Wrap remaining piece of wire around wreath under buttons and wrap ends around pencil to curl.

Step 16. Sew plastic ring to back of Santa, above hat trim, for hanger. $

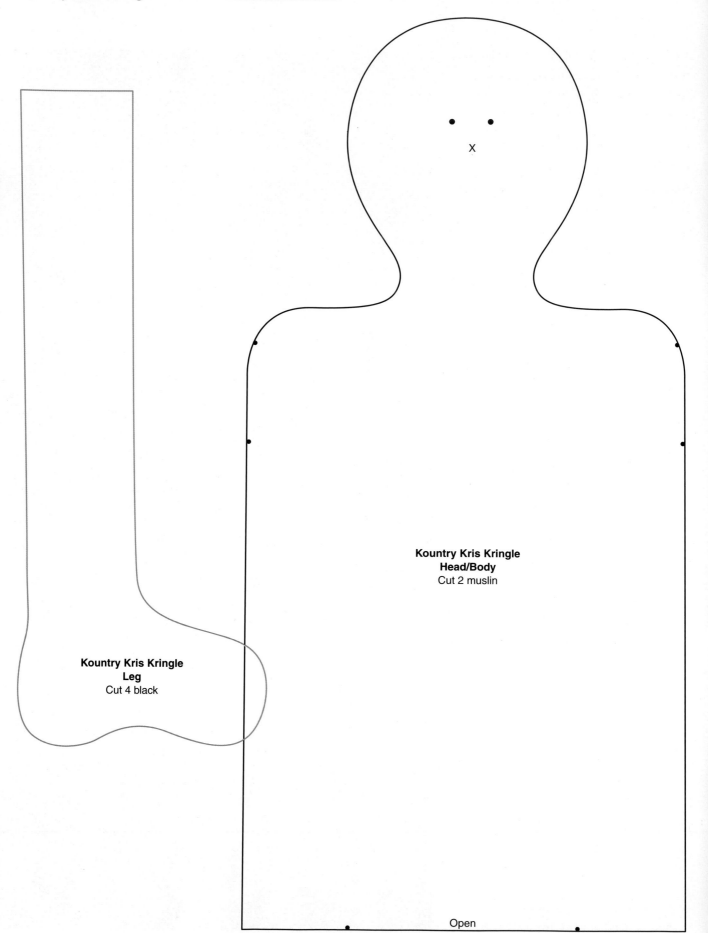

**Kountry Kris Kringle
Head/Body**
Cut 2 muslin

**Kountry Kris Kringle
Leg**
Cut 4 black

X

Open

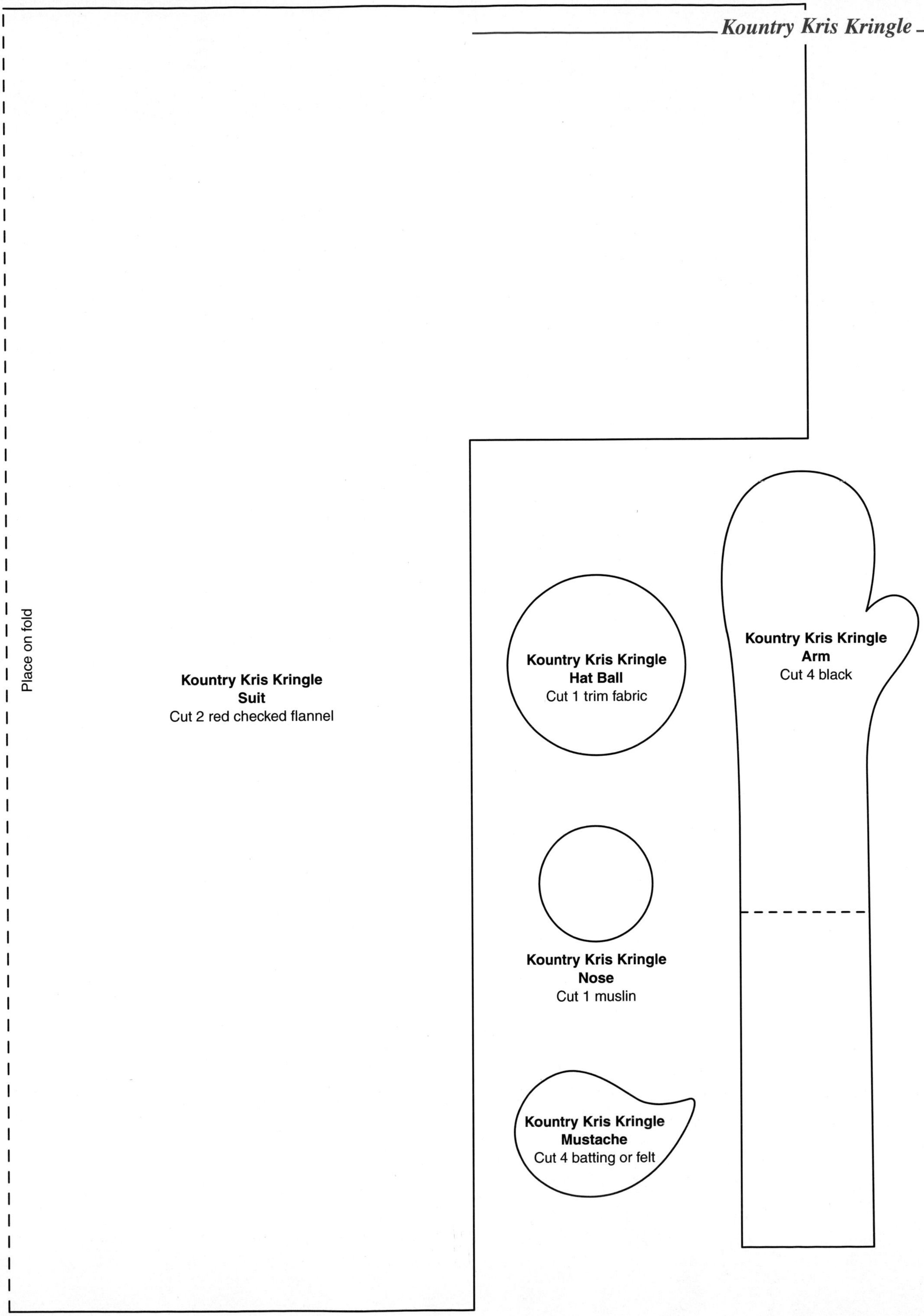

Place on fold

Kountry Kris Kringle
Suit
Cut 2 red checked flannel

Kountry Kris Kringle
Hat Ball
Cut 1 trim fabric

Kountry Kris Kringle
Arm
Cut 4 black

Kountry Kris Kringle
Nose
Cut 1 muslin

Kountry Kris Kringle
Mustache
Cut 4 batting or felt

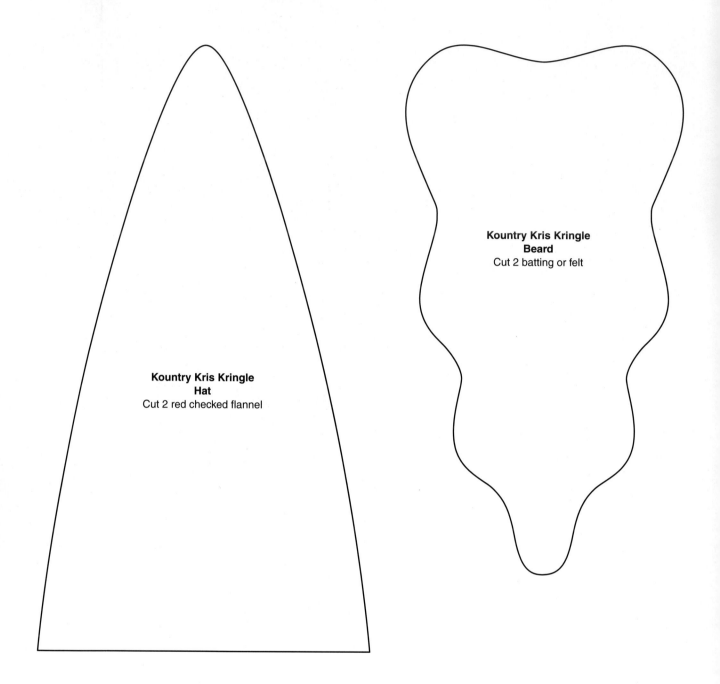

**Kountry Kris Kringle
Hat**
Cut 2 red checked flannel

**Kountry Kris Kringle
Beard**
Cut 2 batting or felt

Teeny-Tiny Snowman Pin

By Mary Ayres

Perfect for the small-gift exchange or for adding a special touch to a package.

Project Specifications

Skill Level: Beginner

Pin Size: Approximately 2¼" x 3¼"

Materials

- 4" white fabric circle
- 3" x 6" blue fabric rectangle
- 1½" white felt circle
- 9 (5mm) black beads for eyes and mouth
- ¼ yard ⅜"-wide silver wire-edged ribbon
- 1 (⁹⁄₁₆") red flat button
- 1 (½") orange pompom for nose
- All-purpose threads to match fabrics
- 2 (1") silk holly leaves
- Polyester fiberfill
- 1½" pin back fastener
- Cosmetic blush
- Cotton swab
- Basic sewing supplies and tools

Instructions

Step 1. Sew a basting stitch close to the edge around 4" white fabric circle. Pull basting stitches tightly to gather, leaving a 1" opening. Stuff circle firmly with polyester fiberfill and flatten.

Step 2. Sew 1½" white felt circle to center back of head, covering fabric circle opening.

Step 3. Sew orange pompom to center of face. Sew two 5mm black beads to face ⅛" above nose and with ⅛" of space between. Sew seven remaining beads under nose for mouth, referring to photo for placement. Leave ⅛" space between each bead. Sew through entire thickness of head when attaching pompom and beads.

Step 4. Fringe long sides of blue fabric for hat using a straight pin to pull one or two threads from edge. Sew short sides of blue fabric rectangle together with ¼" seam, which is center back of hat. Turn right side out. Sew a basting stitch around hat ½" from top edge. Pull basting stitches tightly to gather; knot. Fold bottom of hat up ½" for brim. Put hat on head and stitch in place to secure.

Step 5. Sew silk holly leaves, ends together, to hat brim on right front side.

Step 6. Tie silver wire-edged ribbon in a bow and shape. Trim bow ends even. Sew bow on top of leaves where they are joined. Sew red flat button to center of bow.

Step 7. Sew pin back fastener to center back of hat. Blush cheeks using cotton swab and cosmetic blush. $

Glistening Snowflake Sweatshirt Cardigan

By Mary Ayres

Add some silver sparkle to an ice-blue sweatshirt for a dress-up version of our favorite winter topper.

Project Specifications

Skill Level: Beginner

Cardigan Size: Any Size

Materials

- Woman's ice-blue sweatshirt, any size
- ⅜ yard white-on-white fabric for snowflakes and binding
- 12 sets of 6 (⁵⁄₁₆"–½") white flat buttons
- 6 (¼"–⅜") assorted white buttons
- 2 skeins silver metallic pearl cotton
- White all-purpose thread
- Scraps of fusible transfer web
- Basic sewing supplies and tools

Instructions

Step 1. Cut ribbed edge from bottom of sweatshirt and sleeves.

Step 2. Cut sweatshirt down center front.

Step 3. Measure around bottom of sweatshirt. From white-on-white fabric cut a 2" strip by that measured length, piecing if necessary. Pin to bottom edge of sweatshirt, right sides together and raw edges aligned. Sew ½" from edge. Turn other edge of strip under ½" and pin to back of sweatshirt edge. Stitch in place by hand.

Step 4. Measure center front opening and add 1". From white-on-white fabric cut two strips 2" by that measurement. Sew to sweatshirt front openings as in Step 3, ends extending ½" past neck and bottom edges of cardigan. Turn extended edges under when folding strip to back.

Step 5. Measure sleeve edge and add 1". From white-on-white fabric cut two strips 2" by that measured length. Sew to sleeve edges as in Steps 3 and 4, encasing raw edges in binding.

Step 6. Trace snowflake appliqué shapes on paper side of fusible transfer web as instructed on pattern. Cut out leaving ¼" margin around traced lines. Following manufacturer's instructions fuse to white-on-white fabric. Cut out on traced lines. Referring to photo for placement, arrange on cardigan front and fuse.

Step 7. With silver metallic pearl cotton, work buttonhole stitch around each snowflake piece.

Step 8. Referring to photo as placement guide, transfer snowflake embroidery pattern to cardigan front and sleeves. With silver metallic pearl cotton, embroider snowflakes with stem stitch.

Step 9. Transfer dots around appliqué snowflake for button placement. Arrange two sets of six buttons around each snowflake and sew one of the assorted buttons in the center. Sew buttons in place with silver metallic pearl cotton. $

Glistening Snowflake Sweatshirt Cardigan
Embroidered snowflake pattern

Pattern continued on page 148

Joy Nativity Banner

By Marian Shenk

This night-sky nativity scene has an opulent look with its gold trim and dark colors. Lovely in your own home or that of a family member or friend.

Project Specifications

Skill Level: Beginner

Banner Size: 24½" x 17¾"

Materials

- ½ yard navy metallic print
- ¼ yard royal blue metallic print for borders
- Backing 20" x 26"
- Recycled red Christmas print napkin or red Christmas print fat quarter
- 1 package wide gold metallic bias tape
- Scrap of gold lamé for star
- Scrap of white fleece or felt for nativity
- All-purpose threads to match fabrics
- Gold metallic thread
- Clear nylon monofilament
- Scraps of fusible transfer web
- Gold metallic paint
- Fine paintbrush
- Basic sewing supplies and tools

Instructions

Step 1. From navy metallic print cut one piece 14¼" x 21".

Step 2. From royal blue metallic print cut two strips each 2½" x 18¼" and 2½" x 21". Sew longer strips to top and bottom of rectangle and shorter pieces to sides.

Step 3. With gold metallic thread and decorative machine stitch, sew the wide gold metallic tape over the seams.

Step 4. Cut letters and nativity scene as directed on patterns. Referring to photo, arrange pieces on background. Machine-appliqué nativity scene in place with clear nylon monofilament thread. Machine-appliqué letters with red thread.

Step 5. With gold metallic thread highlight letters by stitching along inside edge of red satin stitch.

Step 6. Trace star on paper side of fusible transfer web. Cut out leaving roughly ½" margin around shape.

Following manufacturer's instructions, fuse to gold lamé. Cut out on traced lines and fuse to banner, referring to photo for placement. Machine-applique around shape with gold metallic thread.

Step 7. Place banner on backing piece and trim backing to same size. Stitch around perimeter with ¼" seam allowance, leaving a 4" opening at the bottom. Turn right side out and press.

Step 8. Transfer star patterns to sky and paint with gold metallic paint.

Step 9. Add sleeve to back for hanging. $

Glistening Snowflake Sweatshirt Cardigan

Continued from page 147

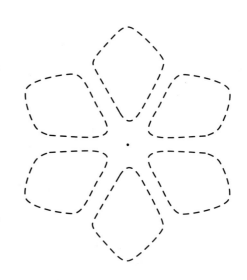

Glistening Snowflake Sweatshirt Cardigan
Appliqué Snowflake
Cut 6 white

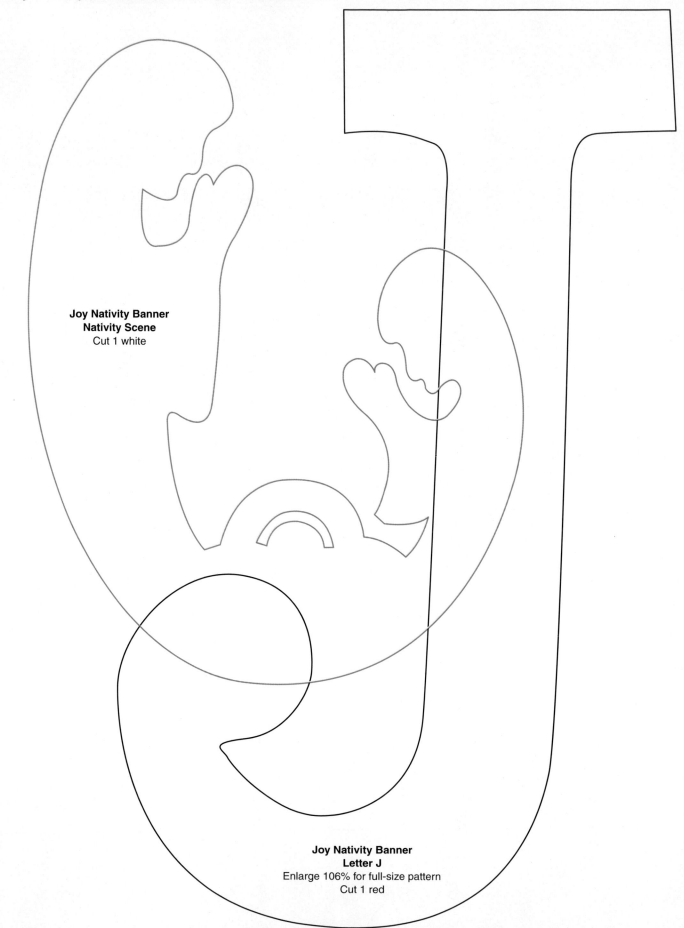

Joy Nativity Banner
Nativity Scene
Cut 1 white

Joy Nativity Banner
Letter J
Enlarge 106% for full-size pattern
Cut 1 red

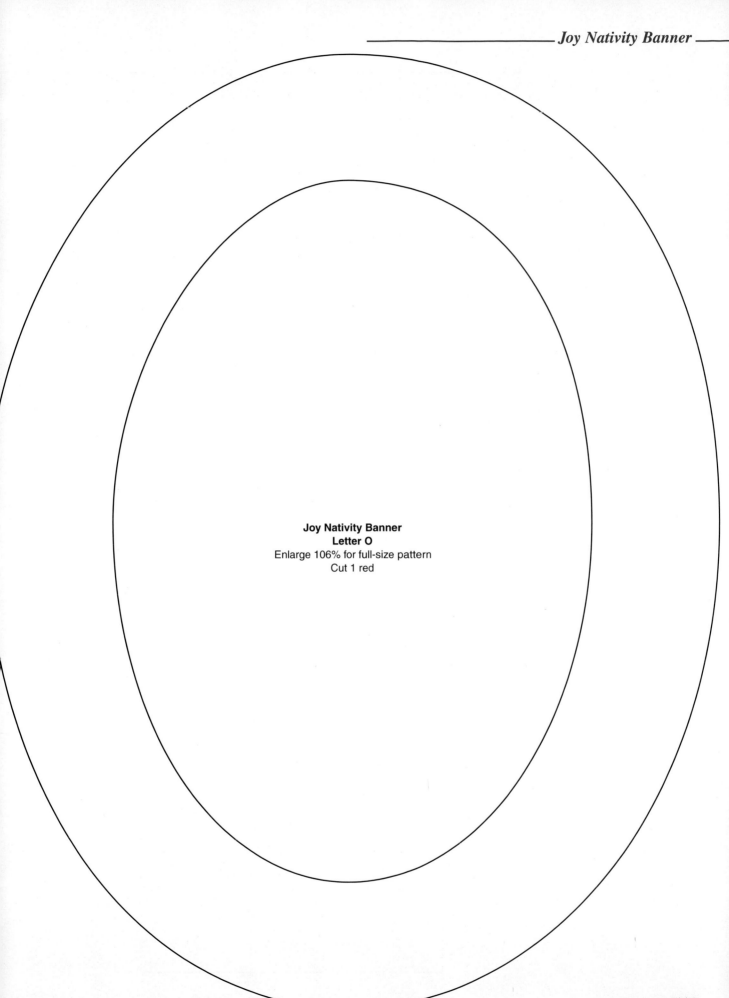

Joy Nativity Banner
Letter O
Enlarge 106% for full-size pattern
Cut 1 red

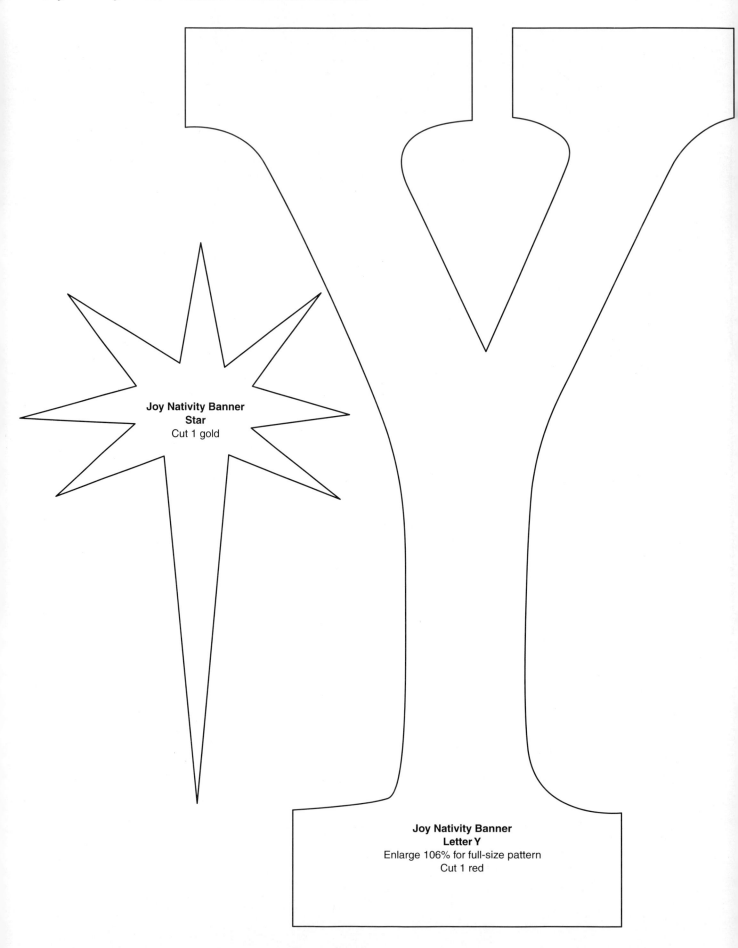

**Joy Nativity Banner
Star**
Cut 1 gold

**Joy Nativity Banner
Letter Y**
Enlarge 106% for full-size pattern
Cut 1 red

Soft & Cheery Snowman

By Mary Ayres

Snowmen are "hot" these days! Everyone is collecting them and this soft, sweet specimen will be "coolest" in your collection.

Project Specifications

Skill Level: Beginner

Snowman Size: Approximately 5½" x 15½"

Materials

- One pair men's white tube socks
- Scrap of orange fabric for nose
- Torn fabric strip 2" x 22" for scarf
- Red, blue and white felt scraps
- Red and silver 6-strand metallic embroidery floss
- 9 (¼") black snaps (all the same side)
- Polyester fiberfill
- Black 6" straw hat
- ⅜ yard (⅜"-wide) silver wire-edged ribbon
- 2 small sprigs of Christmas greenery with red berries
- Poly-pellets for stuffing body
- ½ yard hemp or jute cord
- All-purpose threads to match fabrics
- Pinking shears
- Cosmetic blush
- Cotton swab
- Craft glue
- Basic sewing supplies and tools

Instructions

Step 1. Turn socks wrong side out. Cut one sock horizontally across the tube 13½" up from the toe. Make a 6" vertical cut up the center of the sock through both layers as shown in Fig. 1.

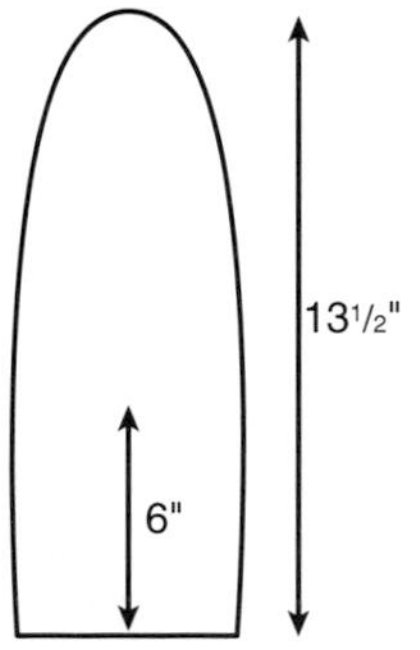

Step 2. Stuff rounded toe end of sock firmly with polyester fiberfill to within 1½" of the 6" split.

Step 3. Separate 6" vertical cut for two legs. Turn raw edges of each leg under ½" and pin, leaving bottom ends open for stuffing. Whipstitch folded edges together with white thread.

Fig. 1
Make 6" vertical cut in sock as shown.

13½"

6"

Step 4. Fill bottom of body cavity with poly-pellets and stitch across top of legs. Fill legs with polyester fiberfill.

Step 5. From white felt cut four 1½" circles. Turn raw edges of ends of legs under ¼". Attach a felt circle to the end of each leg, using 6 strands of silver metallic embroidery floss and buttonhole stitches.

Step 6. To make head, wrap hemp or jute cord around body of sock 3½" down from top of rounded toe end. Pull tightly on cord to make neck indentation and knot to secure.

Step 7. To make arms, cut a 5" square from the remaining sock. Cut the piece in half vertically. Turn raw edges under ¼" and pin, leaving one short side open on each arm for stuffing and attaching felt circles. Whipstitch turned edges together, fill arms with polyester fiberfill and attach felt circles as in Step 5. Sew whipstitched ends of arms to sides of body ½" down from neck.

Step 8. Cut nose from orange fabric. Fold in half and sew straight edges together ⅛" from the edge. Clip corner and turn right side out. Sew a basting stitch around the nose close to the raw edge. Fill nose with polyester fiberfill and pull basting stitch tightly to gather. Knot thread securely. Sew gathered end of nose to center front of face. Bottom of nose should be 1¼" above neck.

Step 9. Blush cheeks with cosmetic blush and cotton swab.

Step 10. Sew two snaps centered above nose for eyes. They should be ¼" above nose with ⅛" of space between them. Referring to photo for placement, sew remaining seven snaps to face for mouth with 3/16" of space between each one.

Step 11. Cut vest pieces as directed on pattern. Sew fronts to back at side and shoulder seams with ¼" seam allowance. Turn vest right side out. Work buttonhole stitch around the front, back and sleeve edges with 6 strands of red embroidery floss. Put vest on showman.

Step 12. Wrap torn fabric strip scarf around snowman's neck, tying it on the right side. Trim scarf ends

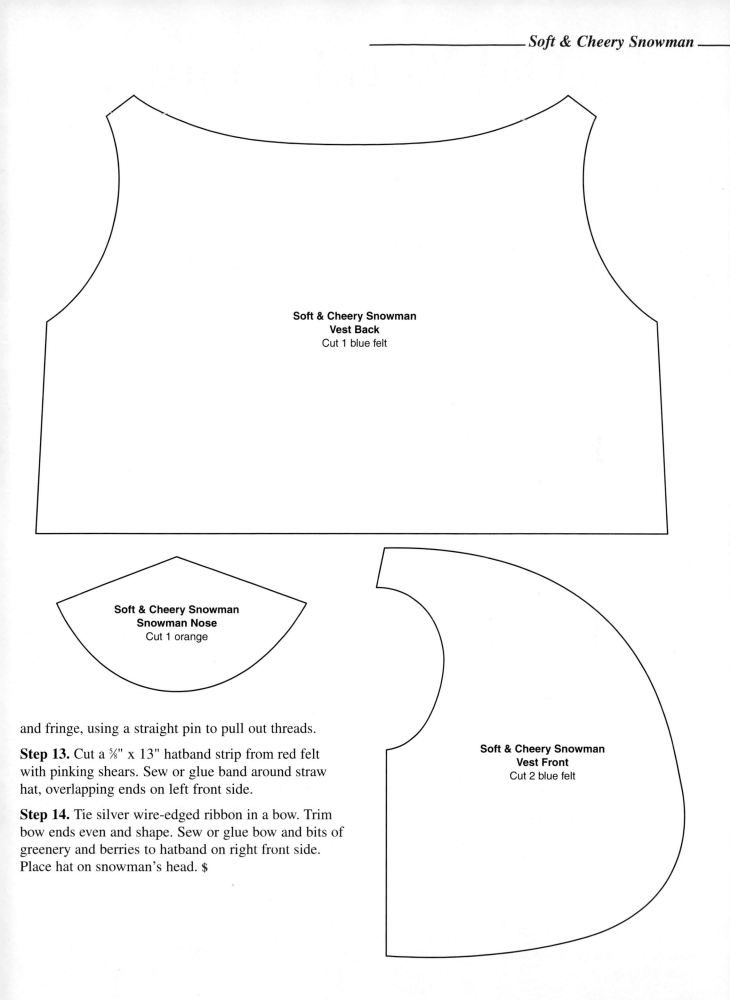

**Soft & Cheery Snowman
Vest Back**
Cut 1 blue felt

**Soft & Cheery Snowman
Snowman Nose**
Cut 1 orange

**Soft & Cheery Snowman
Vest Front**
Cut 2 blue felt

and fringe, using a straight pin to pull out threads.

Step 13. Cut a ⅝" x 13" hatband strip from red felt with pinking shears. Sew or glue band around straw hat, overlapping ends on left front side.

Step 14. Tie silver wire-edged ribbon in a bow. Trim bow ends even and shape. Sew or glue bow and bits of greenery and berries to hatband on right front side. Place hat on snowman's head. $

Old World Santa

By June Fiechter

A Santa of this beauty and elegance will become a family heirloom. The secret of his old-world look and key to economy is recycled fabric. Feel free to change colors according to your "finds."

Project Specifications

Skill Level: Beginner

Santa Size: Approximately 10" x 19"

Materials

- Recycled brown wool blazer
- Recycled burgundy pillow
- Recycled shirt with brown, burgundy and green print
- Scrap of felt 8" x 8" any color
- 8" (¼"-diameter) dowel rod
- Plastic Santa face with chenille beard
- 3" plastic foam ball
- 3½" wreath
- All-purpose threads to match fabrics
- Hot-glue gun and glue
- Sprigs of artificial Christmas floral trim
- 30" cord for belt
- 1 cup weighted material, beans or popcorn for filler
- Basic sewing supplies and tools

Instructions

Step 1. Cut sleeves from blazer and open flat for two rectangles approximately 14" x 16".

Step 2. Sew a long cylinder shape by sewing rectangles together on long edges. Measure diameter of cylinder and cut a circle that size from back of blazer. Sew to bottom of cylinder to make Santa body.

Step 3. Sew a running stitch around top of cylinder for gathering. Pour some weighted material in bottom of body. Remove stuffing from pillow and stuff remainder of cylinder. Pull threads to gather top of body.

Step 4. From recycled shirt cut two pieces each 10" x 12" for sleeves and 8" x 8" for hood. Cut a rectangle 18" x 42", piecing if necessary. Hem one long edge and both short edges. Sew a long running stitch on other long edge for gathering. Pull threads to gather and hot-glue or hand-stitch to top of cylinder with opening at center front.

Step 5. Wrap cord at waist and pull garment up for correct length.

Step 6. Wrap plastic foam ball with 8" felt scrap and hot-glue to back of Santa face.

Step 7. Force dowel rod up through plastic foam ball for neck and down through filler of body. Adjust for proper proportions of body to head and height.

Step 8. Hem one 10" edge of each sleeve piece. Sew 12" edges of each together to make cylinders.

Step 9. Cut mittens as directed on pattern. Right sides together, sew around mittens, leaving wrist edge open. Turn right side out and stuff with small quantity of filler from pillow.

Step 10. Place open end of mitten into hemmed end of sleeves. Position at one edge of sleeve with thumbs up as shown in Fig. 1. Sew over previous hem stitching to close sleeve and attach mitten.

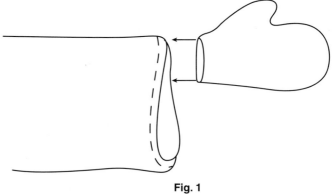

Fig. 1
Position mitten in sleeve as shown.

Step 11. Stuff sleeves lightly with pillow stuffing. Sew open ends together and hot-glue to center back of figure. Be sure thumbs face upward.

Step 12. Hot-glue sprigs of Christmas floral trim to top of wreath. Place wreath in mittened hands and hot-glue in place.

Step 13. Place right sides of 8" x 8" hood squares together and stitch seams on two adjacent sides as shown in Fig. 2 on page 172. Fold back front edges 2" and stitch as shown in Fig. 2 on page 172.

Step 14. Turn hood right side out and cuff the front edge as shown in Fig. 3 on page 172.

Continued on page 172

Wishful Snowman Stocking

By Julie G. DeGroat

Everyone knows it's best to have a great big stocking for stuffing. This one meets that requirement plus it's easy and fun to make in its folk-art style.

Project Specifications

Skill Level: Beginner

Stocking Size: Approximately 11½" x 15"

Materials

- ¼ yard gold felt
- Green felt 8" x 11"
- Scraps of red, white, orange, blue and yellow felt
- Brown, gold and red 6-strand embroidery floss
- 3 (¾") star-shaped craft buttons
- Basic sewing supplies and tools

Instructions

Step 1. Cut out all shapes as indicated on pattern pieces.

Step 2. Arrange pieces on stocking front, referring to photo for placement. Pin in place.

Step 3. Stitch appliqué shapes in place with 2 strands of contrasting embroidery floss. Use both buttonhole and running stitch for variety.

Step 4. For snowman's eye, make French knot with two strands of brown embroidery floss, wrapping thread around needle three times. With same floss color, stitch three tiny running stitches to make mouth. Make running stitches to create path of snowflakes and lazy-daisy stitches for snowman arms.

Step 5. Referring to photo, sew buttons in place.

Step 6. Pin stocking front to stocking back. Use buttonhole stitch and 4 strands of brown embroidery floss to buttonhole-stitch around edges. Leave top open. $

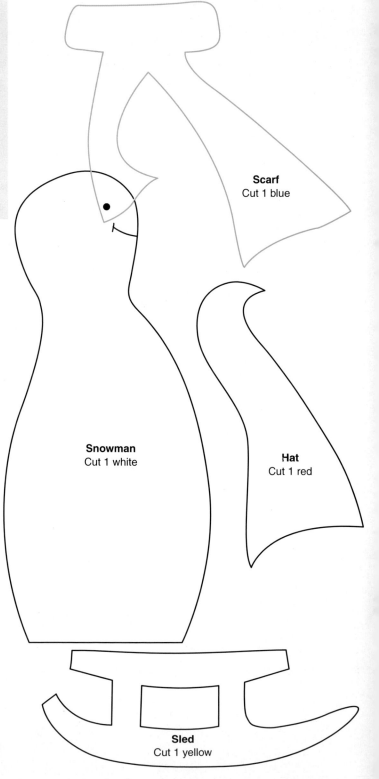

Scarf
Cut 1 blue

Snowman
Cut 1 white

Hat
Cut 1 red

Sled
Cut 1 yellow

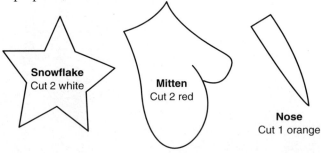

Snowflake
Cut 2 white

Mitten
Cut 2 red

Nose
Cut 1 orange

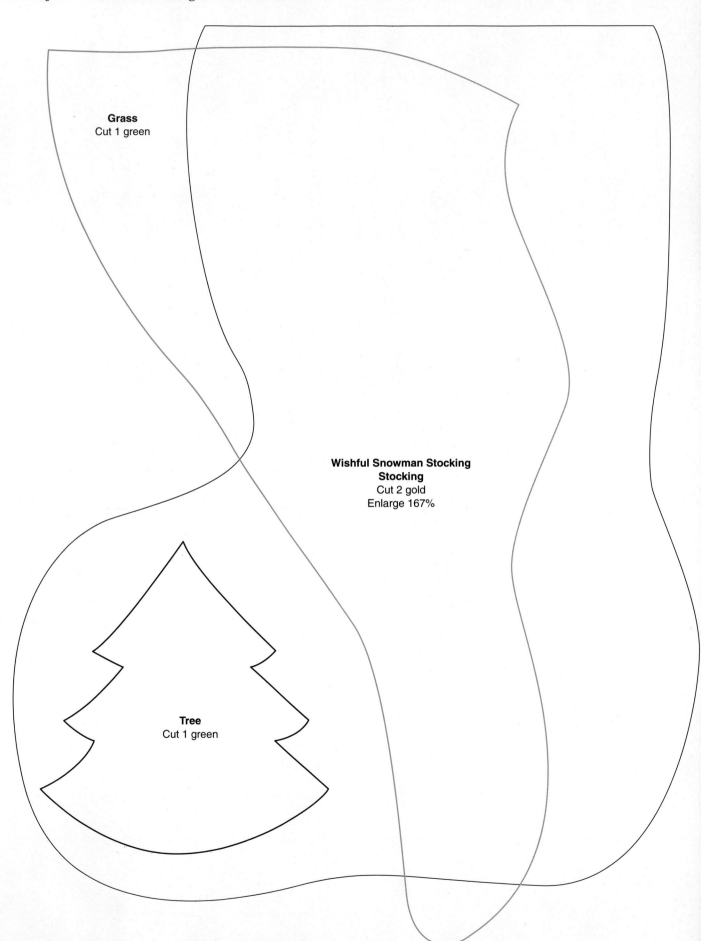

Grass
Cut 1 green

**Wishful Snowman Stocking
Stocking**
Cut 2 gold
Enlarge 167%

Tree
Cut 1 green

Furry Teddy Bear Hat & Scarf

By Janna Britton

This teddy bear accessory set will amuse a little one in your life—sheer fun!

Project Specifications

Skill Level: Beginner

Hat Size: Child Size

Scarf Size: 5" x 44½"

Materials

- 2 craft cuts of cashmere tan plush felt
- 1 square of cocoa brown felt
- ½ yard dark brown print fabric
- ½ yard fusible transfer web
- Low-temperature glue and glue gun
- 1 (1½") black pompom
- 2 (1") black pompoms
- 4 (⅝") black buttons
- 2 (¾") black buttons
- 2 (⅞") brown buttons
- Tan and brown all-purpose thread
- Basic sewing supplies and tools

Instructions

Hat

Step 1. Trace hat and ears on paper side of fusible transfer web as directed on patterns. Cut out leaving roughly ½" margin around traced lines.

Step 2. Following manufacturer's instructions, fuse pieces to wrong sides of dark brown print fabric.

Step 3. Fuse dark brown fabric to wrong side of cashmere tan plush felt. Cut out on traced lines.

Step 4. Wrong sides together, sew four hat pieces together with ¼" seam allowance.

Step 5. Fold ears as marked on pattern. With brown thread, stitch in front of hat side seam. Repeat on other side for second ear.

Step 6. Glue 1½" black pompom in place for nose. From cocoa brown felt cut out mouth and glue in place under nose.

Step 7. Place a ¾" black button on top of a ⅞" brown button. Stitch to hat for eye. Repeat for second eye.

Scarf

Step 1. From cashmere tan plush felt cut two pieces 22½" x 5". Stitch together on two short ends for center back of scarf.

Step 2. Trace two 5" x 22¼" rectangles on paper side of fusible transfer web. Cut out leaving ½" margin around traced lines. Fuse to dark brown print fabric; cut out on traced lines. Fuse to wrong side of cashmere tan plush felt strip. Use scarf curve pattern to trim ends of scarf.

Step 3. Trace ear patterns on paper side of fusible transfer web as instructed on pattern. Cut out leaving roughly ½" margin around traced lines. Fuse to dark brown print fabric and then fuse to wrong side of cashmere tan plush felt. Cut out on traced lines.

Step 4. Fold ears as indicated on pattern and stitch to each side of head at each end of scarf.

Step 5. From cocoa brown felt cut two mouths and glue to face at each end of scarf as indicated on pattern. Glue 1" black pompoms in place for noses.

Step 6. Stitch ⅝" black buttons in place for eyes. **$**

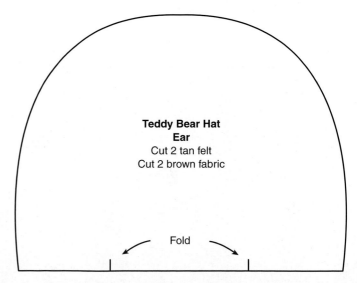

**Teddy Bear Hat
Ear**
Cut 2 tan felt
Cut 2 brown fabric

Fold

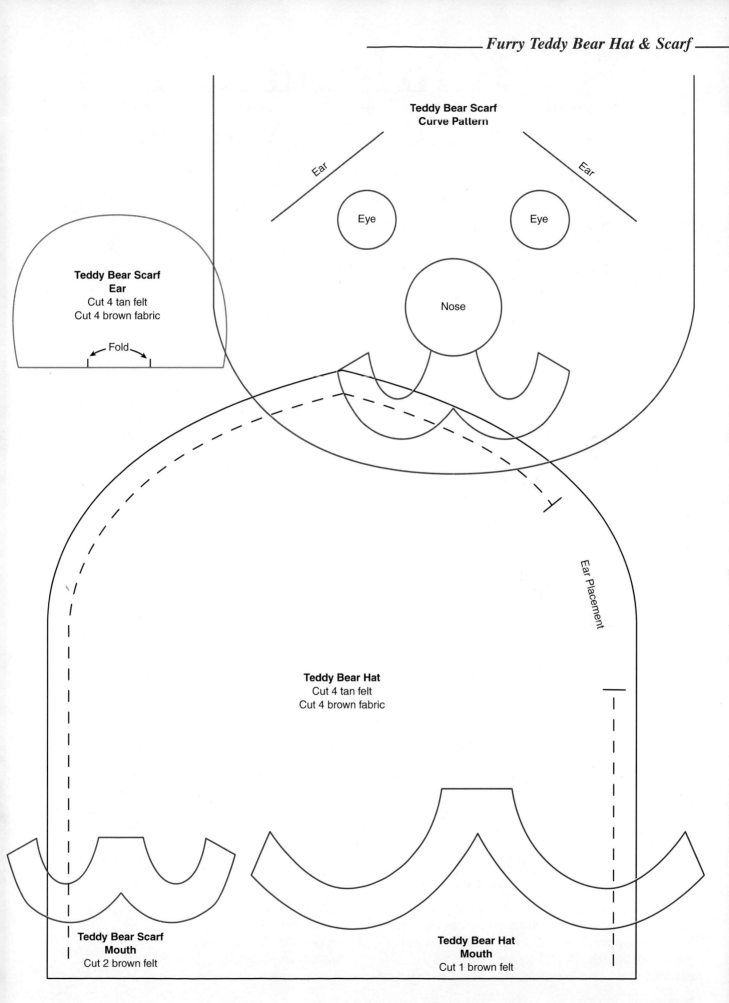

**Teddy Bear Scarf
Curve Pattern**

Ear

Ear

Eye

Eye

Nose

**Teddy Bear Scarf
Ear**
Cut 4 tan felt
Cut 4 brown fabric

Fold

Ear Placement

Teddy Bear Hat
Cut 4 tan felt
Cut 4 brown fabric

**Teddy Bear Scarf
Mouth**
Cut 2 brown felt

**Teddy Bear Hat
Mouth**
Cut 1 brown felt

Christmas Tic-Tac-Toe Game

By Carla Schwab

Start a holiday tradition for any family on your gift list. Tic-tac-toe is a great way for family members of any age to enjoy a challenge while enjoying a few relaxing moments together.

Project Specifications

Skill Level: Beginner

Game Board Size: Approximately 12½" x 12½"

Bag Size: 4¼" x 5½"

Materials

- 1 square each green, burgundy, off-white and tan felt
- 1 fat quarter burgundy print fabric
- 1 fat quarter tan print fabric
- 5 (¾") black flat buttons
- 5 (¾") white flat buttons
- 1 (⅞") black toggle or shank button
- Backing fabric 13" x 13"
- Flat batting 13" x 13"
- Burgundy and brown 6-strand embroidery floss
- 8" (¼"-wide) elastic
- Safety pin
- 10 (⅝") self-adhesive hook-and loop dots
- 2 yards purchased or self-made dark green bias binding
- Burgundy quilting thread
- Basic sewing supplies and tools

Instructions

Game Board

Step 1. From burgundy print fabric cut one square 9½" x 9½".

Step 2. Trace and cut tree from green felt. From tan felt cut one piece 1" x 2" for tree trunk. From burgundy felt cut five 1" x 1" squares. From off-white felt cut four 1" x 1" squares. Referring to photo, arrange pieces on burgundy fabric square; pin. With 2 strands of burgundy embroidery floss, work buttonhole stitch around tree. With brown embroidery floss make multiple

Christmas Tic-Tac-Toe Game
Tree
Cut 1 green felt

rows of running stitches to sew tree trunk to base of tree. Sew 1" squares in place with burgundy running stitch.

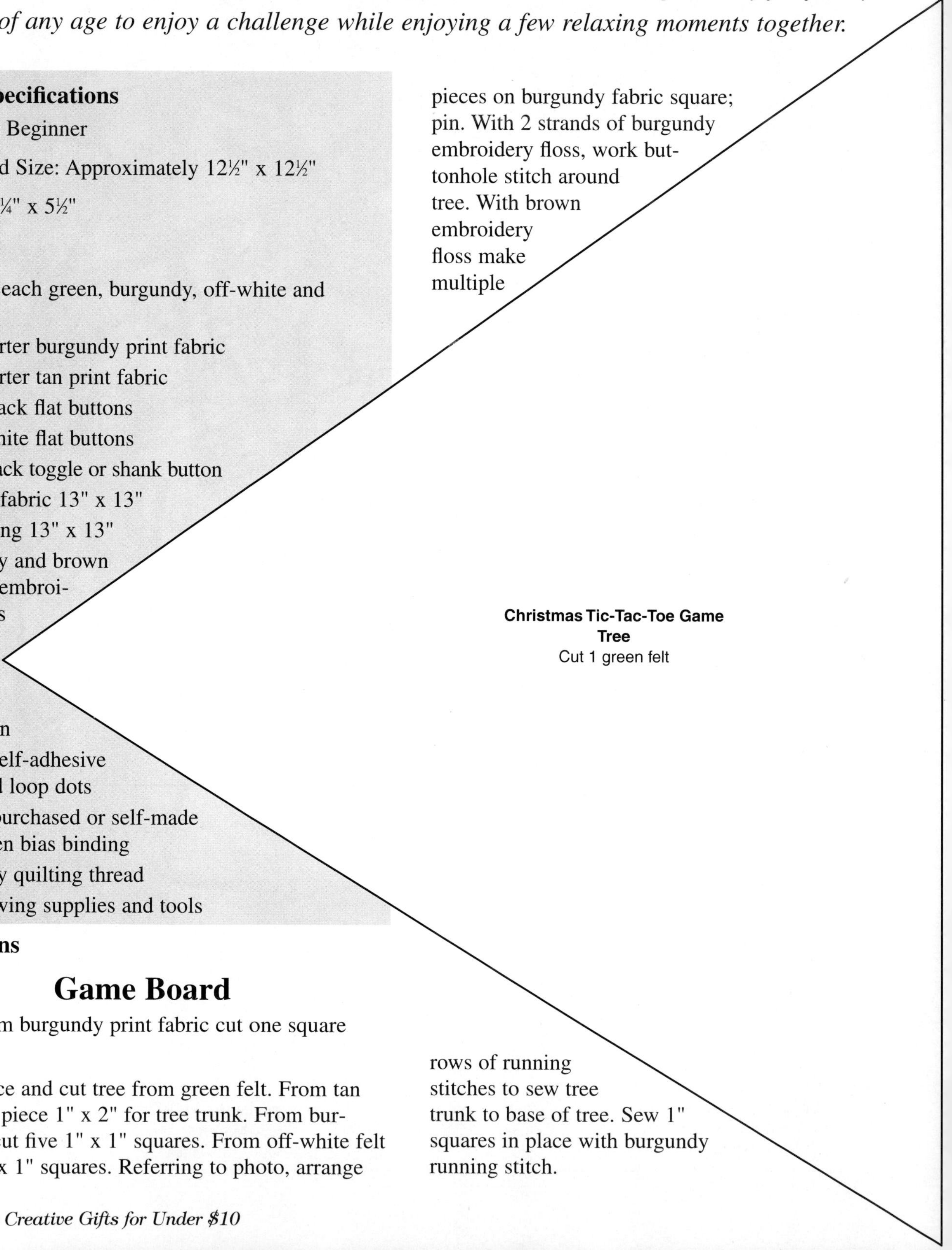

Step 3. From tan print fabric cut two strips each 2" x 9½" and 2" x 12½". Sew shorter strips to sides of game board and longer strips to top and bottom.

Step 4. Baste backing, batting and top layers together. Quilt around tree and trunk, around tic-tac-toe unit and in the ditch along borders with burgundy quilting thread. Trim layers even with top.

Step 5. Bind game board with dark green bias binding.

Step 6. Adhere rough side of hook-and-loop dots to back of five black and five white buttons.

Bag

Step 1. From tan print fabric cut rectangle 7" x 9". Fold in half bringing short sides together. Sew a ¼"

seam along one long and one short edge.

Step 2. Fold remaining raw edge over ¼" and then another 1" to form casing for elastic. Stitch along edge leaving ½" open at seam. Stitch along top of casing ¼" from top of bag.

Step 3. Use safety pin to pull elastic through casing. Draw opening closed to desired tension. Trim excess elastic and sew ends together.

Step 4. Cut a 5" piece of binding. Close fold with stitches and make a loop. Sew to seam inside top of bag.

Step 5. Sew toggle or shank button to upper left corner of game board. Hang bag of checkers on toggle/button by loop. $

Winter Pines Tin Cover & Ornament

By Holly Daniels

This attractive cover dresses up a large coffee tin to make it a wonderful handmade gift container for cookies or other goodies. Tie on the matching ornament as a special bonus.

Project Specifications

Skill Level: Beginner

Tin Cover Size: Fits 36 oz coffee tin

Ornament Size: 3" x 3½"

Materials

- 36 oz coffee tin
- ⅓ yard tan tree-print fabric
- ¼ yard green star-print fabric
- Brown scrap for tree trunks
- 6" strip of hook-and-loop tape
- Scraps of fusible transfer web
- Thin batting 6½" x 21" and 4" x 4½"
- 6 red buttons assorted sizes
- 1 (½"–¾") red star button
- Air-soluble marker
- Pinking shears
- 6" piece of dark green pearl cotton or 6-strand embroidery floss
- Basic sewing supplies and tools

Instructions

Step 1. From tan tree-print fabric cut two rectangles 6½" x 21".

Step 2. Trace appliqué pieces on paper side of fusible transfer web. Cut out leaving roughly ½" margin around pieces. Following manufacturer's instructions, fuse to green star-print and cut out on traced lines.

Step 3. Referring to photo for placement, arrange appliqués on one tan tree-print rectangle; fuse.

Step 4. Place lining tan rectangle face down on work surface. Add batting piece and place appliquéd piece with right side up on top. Pin or baste to secure. Machine-appliqué around each piece with buttonhole or satin stitch.

Step 5. Sew two clusters of three red buttons between appliquéd trees.

Step 6. From green star-print cut two strips each 2" x 21" and 2" x 6½". Fold each strip in half lengthwise, wrong sides together, and press. Bind short ends of appliquéd panel with short strips and long sides with longer strips.

Step 7. Sew one side of hook-and-loop tape to wrong side of one short end of bound panel. Wrap around can and determine placement of second hook-and-loop strip and sew in place.

Ornament

Step 1. From tan tree-print fabric and green star-print fabric cut one piece each 4" x 4½". Trace tree appliqué pattern on tan fabric with air-soluble marker. Layer fabrics with batting, right sides of fabric out.

Step 2. Knot ends of 6" dark green pearl cotton or 6-strand embroidery floss to make circle. Place circle so knot will fall within sewing line of ornament.

Step 3. Sew through all layers with straight stitch.

Step 4. Trim around traced pattern with pinking shears, taking care not to cut hanger.

Step 5. Sew red star button to top of tree. $

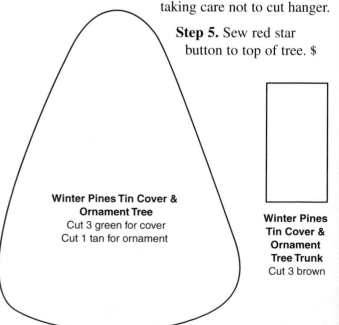

Winter Pines Tin Cover & Ornament Tree
Cut 3 green for cover
Cut 1 tan for ornament

Winter Pines Tin Cover & Ornament Tree Trunk
Cut 3 brown

Gingerbread Play Mat & Finger Puppets

By Connie Matricardi

Hang the play mat on the wall to become a finger-puppet background. At naptime, place it on the bed to occupy little ones as they drift off to sleep, perhaps to dream of sugarplums.

Project Specifications

Skill Level: Beginner

Blanket Size: Approximately 30" x 36"

Materials

- Baby blanket or recycled blanket remnant 30" x 36"
- Red and white felt 9" x 12" each
- Green and brown felt 9" x 12" two each
- All-purpose sewing threads to match fabrics
- 1 package green jumbo rickrack
- 12" length of regular green rickrack
- 12" length of regular red rickrack
- 4 (⅝") hook-and-loop dots
- White dimensional paint pen
- 2 packages extra-wide double-fold bias tape to match blanket remnant
- Basic sewing supplies and tools

Instructions

Step 1. Follow manufacturer's directions to attach double-fold bias tape around perimeter of blanket remnant.

Step 2. Trace and cut felt shapes as directed on patterns.

Step 3. To make finger puppets sew one rough hook-and-loop dot to back of one gingerbread boy shape. Using white thread, sew gingerbread boy front to gingerbread boy back. Sew around perimeter of shape, leaving bottom edge open. Repeat for the second gingerbread boy and for two gingerbread girls.

Step 4. Use white dimensional paint pen to draw eyes and three buttons on each gingerbread figure.

Step 5. Sew red rickrack, small heart and door to gingerbread house.

Step 6. Referring to photo, arrange all felt shapes and green rickrack lengths on blanket surface. Jumbo green rickrack lengths from door to gingerbread figures are approximately 22" and 28". Green rickrack length from chimney is 12".

Step 7. Pin shapes and rickrack in place. Pin four opposite hook-and-loop dots to blanket surface to mark position of finger puppets.

Step 8. Sew all pieces to blanket. Felt shapes should cover all raw edges of rickrack except turn under end from chimney. Choose bobbin thread color to match blanket. Use same bobbin thread throughout project. Change needle thread color when necessary to match color of shapes.

Step 9. Attach finger puppets to blanket. $

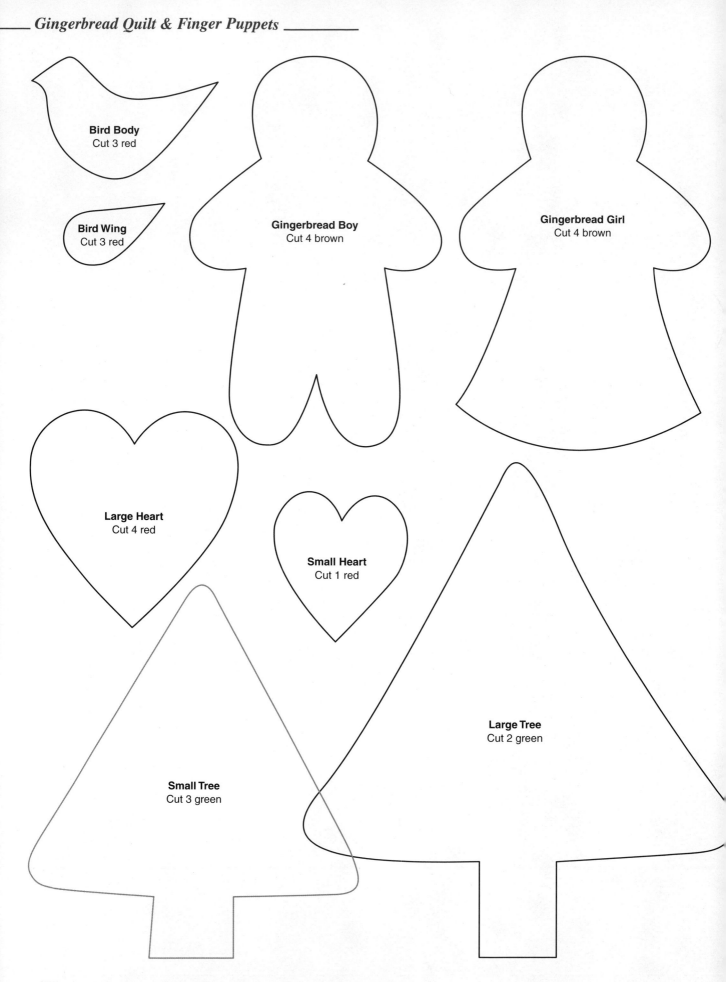

Bird Body
Cut 3 red

Bird Wing
Cut 3 red

Gingerbread Boy
Cut 4 brown

Gingerbread Girl
Cut 4 brown

Large Heart
Cut 4 red

Small Heart
Cut 1 red

Large Tree
Cut 2 green

Small Tree
Cut 3 green

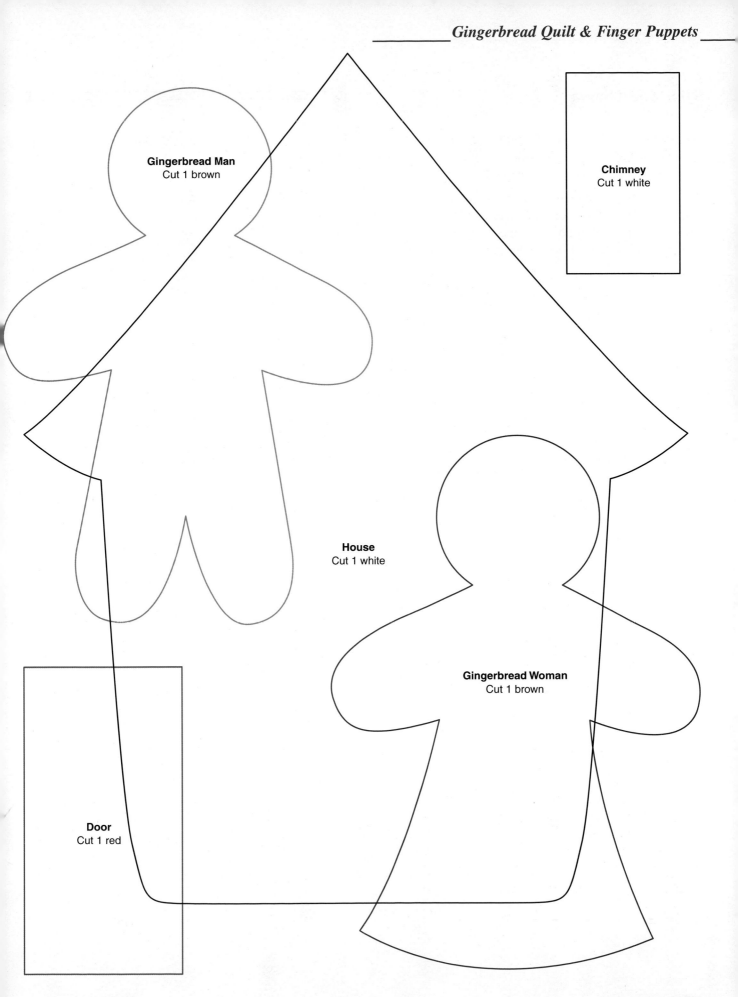

Gingerbread Man
Cut 1 brown

Chimney
Cut 1 white

House
Cut 1 white

Gingerbread Woman
Cut 1 brown

Door
Cut 1 red

Old-World Santa

Continued from page 156

Step 15. Place hood over plastic foam ball and hot-glue raw edges of hood at neck. Hot-glue front of hood to face and beard to hide ball.

Step 16. Cut pillow seams and create a 19" x 35" cape rectangle. Hem two short ends and one long edge. Sew a long running stitch on raw edge. Pull threads to gather and hot-glue at neck edge. $

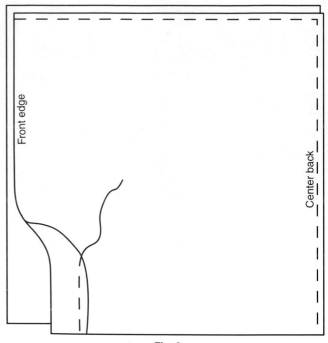

Fig. 2
Stitch seams on 2 adjacent sides of
hood. Fold back 2" at front edge and stitch.

**Old World Santa
Mitten**
Cut 4 (reverse 2)

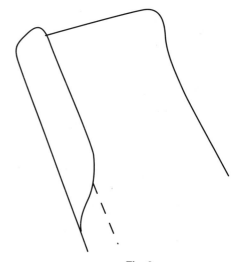

Fig. 3
Cuff front edge of hood as shown.

Sewing Guidelines

Basic Sewing Supplies

- Sewing machine
- Sharp scissors or shears
- Straight pins
- Hand-sewing needles
- Thimble (optional)
- Seam ripper
- Chalk marker or fade-out pen (for temporary marks)

An iron and ironing board, although not strictly sewing tools, are essential to great-looking projects. Don't be afraid to use them liberally!

Handmade Stitches

Buttonhole Stitch

(Sometimes called blanket stitch)

Working left to right, bring needle up at A, down at B and up at C with thread below needle. Stitches should be evenly spaced and of a consistent depth.

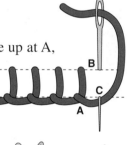

French Knot

Bring the needle up through the fabric. Point the needle at yourself, then wrap the thread or floss clockwise around the needle. Insert the needle back down through the fabric one thread away from the exit point.

Lazy-Daisy Stitch

Bring needle up through fabric at A, make a loop and hold it with your thumb. Insert the needle back down through fabric at A and up at B. Make a small anchor stitch to hold the loop in place.

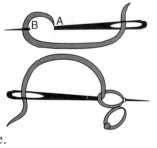

Slip Stitch

Slip stitches are worked by hand to make an almost invisible finish.

1. Work with a single thread along two folded edges.

2. Insert needle in one fold and slide a short distance.

3. Pick up a thread from the other folded edge and slip point of needle back in first fold.

4. Repeat (slide, pick up thread, insert back in first fold) along length of opening.

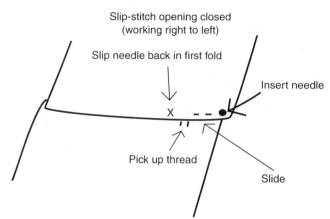

Slip-stitch opening closed (working right to left)

Slip needle back in first fold

Insert needle

Pick up thread

Slide

5. Bury knot between folds.

Straight Stitch

The basis of many hand-embroidery stitches, the straight stitch is formed by bringing the needle up at A and down at B.

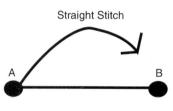

Straight Stitch

Satin Stitch

Satin stitches are simply straight stitches worked very closely together to fill in a solid shape. That shape is sometimes outlined for additional definition. ***Note:*** *Threads should lie closely side by side, but not overlapping.*

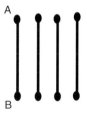

Satin Stitch

Enlarging Patterns

There are several ways to enlarge patterns—all of which are perfectly acceptable. Please choose the method that works best for you.

Photocopy

Photocopy the pattern provided at a copy shop at the percentage enlargement you want (100 percent is the size of the original; 150 percent is 1½ times the original; 200 percent is twice the size of the original, etc). If the shopkeeper objects, due to copyright infringement, tell him you have permission from the publisher to make one copy so you don't have to cut the book (show him this note, if necessary).

Grid Pattern

Any pattern can also be enlarged using a grid pattern. Draw a grid on the pattern every ½". Then, draw 1" grid on a piece of tracing paper or other lightweight paper. The final step is to transfer the lines in each grid from the pattern to the 1" grid. This is equal to photocopying the pattern at 200 percent.

Transferring Patterns

There are several methods for transferring pattern outlines and details. Choose the one that works best for your project.

Outline Pattern

1. Place tracing paper over pattern in book or magazine.

2. Trace with pencil; cut out with scissors.

3. Place pattern on the project. Pin in place, then cut or draw around the periphery.

Graphite Paper

When details need to be transferred as well as the pattern outline:

1. Place tracing paper over pattern in book or magazine.

2. Trace with pencil, but do not cut out.

3. Place pattern on the project; insert graphite or transfer paper between the project and pattern with the media side toward the fabric.

4. Retrace design lines with a dried-out ball point pen to transfer lines to fabric.

Iron-on Transfer Pencil

Another method for transferring pattern details:

1. Place tracing paper over pattern in book or magazine.

2. Trace with pencil, but do not cut out.

3. Turn paper over; trace detail lines with an iron-on transfer pencil.

4. Place pattern on the project with the media side toward the fabric.

5. Apply heat with an iron, following manufacturer's directions to transfer marks to fabric.

Satin Stitch by Machine

Machine-made satin stitches are often used to finish appliqué pieces and consist of closely worked zigzag stitches.

Stitch Size

The width and length of the stitches are determined by the size of the appliqué and the body of the fabric.

1. Small appliqué pieces call for narrow zigzag stitches.

2. Large appliqué pieces call for wider zigzag stitches.

3. Fragile or brittle fabrics, such as metallics,

lamés, sheer organza, etc., require longer stitches to prevent damaging fibers and effectively "cutting" the appliqué piece out of the background.

4. Fuzzy fabrics, such as shaggy felt or synthetic fur, require wider stitches and a medium width.

Threads

Threads used for satin-stitch appliqué are chosen for their weight, color and finish.

1. For fine fabrics, those with small woven threads, choose a fine thread, such as silk, rayon, or thin cotton. Machine embroidery threads are a good choice.

2. For medium-weight fabrics, a medium-weight rayon or cotton thread works nicely. Threads in variegated colors add interest.

3. Heavy-weight fabrics might do well with a heavy-duty thread worked in a buttonhole stitch, rather than satin stitch.

4. Test threads of different weights and finishes on a sample of the fabrics in your project before making the final choice.

5. Select threads in coordinating or contrasting colors, as desired.

Helpful Tips

1. Thread upper machine with rayon thread and bobbin with a cotton or cotton-wrapped polyester thread in a color neutral to the backing, if the back will show. Or, chose a cotton or cotton-wrapped polyester thread in the same color used on the top if the backing will not be visible in the completed project.

2. Loosen the top tension slightly. This pulls the loop of the stitch to the back for a smooth look on the top.

3. When turning inside corners, stop with the needle down in the fabric on the inside (see Fig. 1).

4. When turning outside corners, stop with the needle down in the fabric on the outside (see Fig. 2).

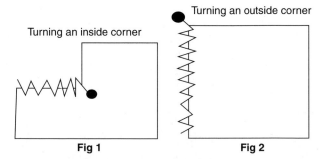

Turning an inside corner — **Fig 1**

Turning an outside corner — **Fig 2**

5. If the machine is skipping stitches:

• Clean the machine thoroughly, removing any build-up of fuzz beneath the feed dogs.

- Use a new needle.
- Try a needle of a different size.
- Match size and point of needle to the thread and fabric in the project.
- Apply a silicone needle lubricant to the needle, thread, and every place the thread touches the machine in the upper threading track.

6. An iron-on, tear-away stabilizer seems like an unnecessary purchase, but what it adds to the quality of a machine-appliquéd project cannot be denied. The product is ironed on the wrong side of the fabric under the area to be appliquéd. This keeps it from shifting during machine-stitching. When the work is done, the stabilizer is simply torn away. A touch of the iron adds the finishing touch for an appliqué project free of lumps and bumps!

Tea-Dyeing Fabric

Fabric can be dyed in a bath of strong tea to give it an aged effect.

1. Wet the fabric in clear water; squeeze excess moisture from fabric, but do not wring or twist.

2. Immerse in a hot bath of water and several tea bags. Allow to soak for 20–30 minutes.

3. Remove fabric; squeeze excess moisture out.

4. Hang fabric to dry, or dry in dryer.

Helpful Tips

- Fabric will dry lighter than it appears when wet.
- Conservationists warn that tannic acid in such a tea bath will cause damage to fabrics over a period of years, so this method should not be used on an heirloom project.
- 100-percent cotton muslin or broadcloth works best.

Gathering Stitches by Hand

Work a long running stitch close to the edge of the piece to be gathered with a doubled thread. Pull gently to gather. If fabric is heavy, use heavy-duty thread, such as carpet thread.

Gathering Stitches by Machine

To work gathering stitches by machine, set the sewing machine for the longest stitch possible (some newer machines have a built-in basting stitch). Pull the bobbin thread firmly and evenly to gather.

If the fabric is heavy, work a medium zigzag stitch over a strand of thin crochet thread. Then, pull the crochet thread to gather.

Topstitching Trims by Machine

Rickrack

To attach narrow rickrack by machine, run a straight stitch down the center of the trim. To attach wide rickrack, work a zigzag stitch or a broken zigzag along length of the trim.

Piping

To attach piping, baste close to the piping (use a zipper foot, if necessary) on one piece of the project with raw edges even. Place the other piece on the project, with right sides together, and stitch along the basting stitches through all layers of the project.

Cording

To attach cording or other narrow trims, work a zigzag stitch slightly wider than the trim with monofilament thread (for an invisible stitch) or with decorative threads for an embellished look.

Using Fusible Web

There is more than one kind of fusible web! The light or ultra-light versions have less adhesive on them and will accept machine stitches. The heavy-duty versions have a thicker layer of adhesive and are designed to be used without machine stitches. In fact, if you try to sew through the heavy-duty kind, the adhesive gums up the needle and causes a mess.

The best advice is to read the manufacturer's directions. Each manufacturer has a different formula for the adhesive and may require different handling.

Regardless of the type fusible product you choose, they may all be applied to fabric in generally the same way.

Fusible Appliqué

1. Trace the desired motif on paper side of the adhesive with a marking tool (pen, pencil, permanent marker, etc.).

2. Cut out around the marks, leaving a margin.

3. Bond the fusible web to the wrong side of desired fabric.

4. Cut through fabric, web and paper backing, following the drawn shape.

5. Remove paper backing and place the shape on desired background.

6. Fuse in place, following manufacturer's directions.

7. Finish edges with machine-worked stitches or fabric paint, if desired.

Special Thanks

We would like to thank the talented designers whose work is featured in this collection.

Mary Ayres
Vintage Valentine, 10
Buttoned-up Heart Sachets, 20
Woven Heart Pillow, 14
Spring Is Sprung Wall Quilt, 42
Fanciful Fish Place Mat &
    Napkin Ring, 72
Sunflower Buttons Pillow, 74
Playful Pals Bibs, 101
Chubby Ducky, 100
Falling Leaves Pot Holders, 118
Friendly Frankie Trick-or-Treat
    Bag, 120
Miss Witch, 122
Berry Christmas Towel, 139
Teeny Tiny Snowman Pin, 145
Glistening Snowflake Sweatshirt
    Cardigan, 146
Soft & Cheery Snowman, 153

Janna Britton
Patched-up Heart, 32
Johnny's Apple Trail, 133
Mosaic Leaves Basket Topper, 126
Festive Holiday Basket, 138
Furry Teddy Bear Hat & Scarf, 161

Holly Daniels
Hearts Entwined, 8
Winter Pines Tin Cover &
    Ornament, 166
Pretty Floral Bath Set, 85

Julie DeGroat
Bushel of Apples Pincushions, 112
Wishful Snowman Stocking, 158

June Fiechter
Birthday Cupcake Surprise Bag, 30
Teatime Pot Holders, 48
Strawberry Fluff Pillow, 44
Sweet Little Ladybug Dress Set, 63
Pretty as a Picture, 108
Pumpkin-Patch Car Coat, 128
Old World Santa, 156

Donna Friebertshauser
Smocked Gingham Garden Hat, 62

Lisa Galvin
Now Playing—A Party Just for You!, 24

Cindy Gorder
Pocketful of Love, 34
Beaded Lavender Sachets, 78
Sewing Treasures Gift Set, 82

Cathy Hallier
Pocket Pal Coin Purses, 95

Thaea Lloyd
Pretty Posies Pillow, 90

Chris Malone
Cheery Checks Catch-All, 12
"Boy … Am I Stuffed"
    Wall Hanging," 23
Birthday Boy & Birthday Girl
    Gift Bags, 28
Bunny Flight Basket, 40
Kountry Kris Kringle, 140

Connie Matricardi
Gingerbread Play Mat & Finger
    Puppets, 168

Karen Mead
Heirloom Lace Pillow, 19
Reader's Pillow, 47
Victorian Sachet Slippers, 92
Embellished Closet Safe, 96
Baby's Toy Bag, 104
Halloween Hugs, 116

Patsy Moreland
Soft Floral Gift Box, 80
Denim Totes, 88

Debbie Roney
Double-Dip Delight, 36
Pumpkins on the Vine, 132

Judith Sandstrom
Dolly and Me Jumpers, 54

Carla Schwab
Christmas Tic-Tac-Toe Game, 164

Marian Shenk
Bunny Tote, 51
Summer Garden Snack Trays &
    Coaster Set, 70
Joy Nativity Banner, 148

Julie Weaver
Homespun Charm Kitchen Towels, 67
Baby Blocks Bib, 106
Autumn Breeze Sweatshirt Jacket, 113

Angie Wilhite
Sown With Love, 16